20-Nothings

stories on surviving the most significant,
least important decade of my life

jessie rosen

Copyright © 2013 Jessie Rosen

All rights reserved.

ISBN-13: 978-1490377346

For R, the source of all my best ideas

CONTENTS

Acknowledgments	i
The Original Blog Intro	3
Deeb the Dealbreaker	5
A Gift From My God	7
To Choose a Choice	11
Well…We're GChatting	15
My Stab at The/A "One"	19
Parents Are People Too	23
What's Your Scary Age?	27
You Know You're Not In College When	31
Go To A Bar Alone	35
I Grew Up A Little Bit On Sunday Around 8:30PM	39
A Modern Meet Cute Theory	43
My 80-Year Old Dentist on Online Dating	47
Adopt-A-Boyfriend	51

When It Becomes Riskier To Not Go After The Girl	55
Aluminum Magnolias	59
How And Why Rachel Is Never Single	63
My Mom, Me and Choice	67
How To Go From Friends To More Than Friends	71
Phone Calls: Chivalry or Pleated Pants	75
An Open Letter To Anyone About To End A Relationship	79
Kennedy and the Case of the Superior Set-up	83
The Bullshit of Opportunity Cost	87
What I'm Worth To The Men of Murray Hill	91
I'm Moving Out To Move Up	95
What I Learned At My Five Year Reunion	99
My Busband and Me	103
On Being Mayor of a Non-existent Town	107
I'm Officially My Scary Age	111

It's Time To Tell The Blog	115
It's Not You, Armin, It's My New Overwhelming Life	121
California Culture Shock	125
Surviving My First Mini Trip As A Couple	129
My Car Battery & My Status As A Woman	133
The Long Overdue Story of How R and I Met	137
I've Become The Girlfriend I Hate	143
Graduating For the Third Time	147
Letting My Freak Flag Fly: Suitcase Edition	151
The Annual Birthday Blog Post	155
Relationship Advice From Yet Another Dentist	159
This Is Exactly What Happens When You Go For Your First Mammogram	161
How To Prepare To Move In With Your Boyfriend	165
My Secret, Special Birthday Routine	169
Today Is My 29th Birthday, and I feel…	173

Why I Haven't Written Lately and What It's Made Me Realize	175
Dating Advice for Baby Zadie	181
Today Is The Last Day of My Current Life	185
10 Things Every Almost 30-Year Old Woman Should Be Able to Say	187
Why I Was So Sure The Answer to "Will You Marry Me" Should Be Yes!	189
How Registering For Wedding Gifts is Nothing Like Shopping For Shoes	193
Dating Rules From My Future Self	197
Current Plans for My Future Rich Old Lady Self	201
The Final Word On: Hooking Up	205
The Final Word On: Dating	209
How To Survive Your 20's	211

ACKNOWLEDGMENTS

An endless number of people have been part of this six year writing experience – from family members and mentors to random readers and trusted friends - far too many to mention individually. But I do need to say *thank you* to the one person who started it all in the first place.

You were right, Pierson. This blog was a really good idea.

Desperate Times, Online Measures

from 10/6/07

We thought we had it all figured out. Until we discovered we hated our job after the first month, and a co-worker asked us out on a date, and we had to decide if "adult" hook-ups always include sex, and our first check bounced. That's when we realized we were screwed. No more dorm living room forums, no more focus-on-your-life-goals courses, drafts that cost way more than a dollar. Just us, out there, trying to figure this shit out over quick Gchat sessions while the boss isn't looking.

We figure the feeling is mutual. Our remedy: sarcastic griping about the hard-hitting issues of our 20's to provide some much-needed comfort and, hopefully, a laugh or two. Mostly, we're just trying to re-create the magic of our senior year lunch table inside the famed Boston College Eagles Nest dining hall – the place where all issues, big or small, came to be mulled over, laughed about, and put to rest over the course of our daily, 3-hours meals. Pull up a chair. We've got 5 + years.

Ed Note: These were the very first words that I ever wrote for 20-Nothings.com. The "we" was my friend Matt Pierson and I, the intended writers. Pierson dropped off soon after, at which point the blog became mostly about what to wear and how to find men who care about it, etc. Still, I don't think I'd change anything about this intro today – well, except for the 5+ years to go part. I'd like to extend that by, say, 5+ years.

What follows are posts written throughout the six years that I continued on with 20-Nothings. I tried to pick stories that felt important or inspiring, but I ended up going with the ones that make me laugh the most. I hope you'll enjoy reading them as much as I enjoyed living them – that as all the ones that don't involve me getting dumped.

jessie rosen

Deeb the Dealbreaker

from 12/19/07

My girls and I play a little game we call Deal Breakers. It's simple. We go through the alphabet and assign one deal-breaker quality - something that would end a potential relationship with a guy- to each letter. A: acne, B: bald, C: cancer...and it goes on. It is a rousing game that results in heated discussion and, sometimes, hurt feelings.

- "T: tattoo?! You're saying you couldn't be with someone who has a tattoo?! That's so closed-minded!"

- "U is for Uniform? Wait – like any kind of uniform? Like, postal worker, military person, fireman? That's ridiculous. You just don't want to say B: blue collar."

- "Yes, C: Cancer. I'm saying I wouldn't start a relationship with someone currently battling cancer. Sorry. I stand by that."

I'll spare you my entire alphabet. Let's just say Deeb the man who sells me my falafels was out on enough letters to make for a nice Scrabble turn – or entire game.

I'll clarify, Deeb my falafel man is the 26-year-old son of Sam, the owner of Sam's Falafel, the spot three doors down from my apartment that I stop by most - no - every time I come home drunk.

Deeb took the business over from his father Sam as a change from his years on Wall Street, years he spent making dough (figurative) so he could invest in real estate and continue building his family business. His family, Syrian immigrants, has owned

Sam's Falafel and a number of surrounding properties for decades. Deeb intends to help his father for several years before returning to his own real estate investments and opening a bar or restaurant of his own. It's a real American success story.

Apparently over the past four or five months of my drunkenly stumbling into Sam's Falafel, Deeb has taken a liking to me. This I cannot explain, mostly because I only remember about 30% of the details of our dozens of meetings. Apparently I'm blackout charming.

Whatever the reasons, Deeb has officially asked me out for a drink, and I am officially torn. Do I break my own deal breaker and go? Crazy-strong New York accent…dozens of tattoos…lives with his parents…has only ever seen me between the hours of 12 and 3AM? I can't say I see this going far. Then again, weren't deals meant to be broken? Or was that rules…

Ed Note: My non-relationship with Deeb continued for the four years that I lived on Thompson Street despite the fact that we never went on an official date – unless you consider me sitting on a milk carton in the back kitchen while Deeb made me his special Syrian French fries a date. I might in light of what else was going on in my dating life at the time.

Years after I left Thompson Street, I ran into Deeb inside the lobby of a slick downtown property. Apparently he'd made good on his promise of leaving the family business to continue in his real estate pursuits. He was charming, as always, but this time his black suit and lack of dirty white apron made me wonder if I made a big mistake all those years back. Then he looked at me with longing in his eyes and said, "Oh man, remember that time your falafel exploded onto that little black thing you were wearing but you just kept on eating?? That was so hot." I think things worked out just right, deal or no deal.

A Gift From My God

from 2/7/08

Today was the most significant day of my recent life. No sarcasm. No exaggeration.

To provide some perspective, in my recent life – say 1 to 1.5 years – I have gotten a new job, been promoted at that job, begun life-changing friendships, ended life-changing friendships, switched entirely to skinny jeans, and run four miles without stopping. It's been a big year. Today, however, topped it all. Today I found out that I can stay in my current apartment and take over the lease from my former roommate without the rent being raised to market value or having to pay the new-renter's fee of two months rent.

If you've never lived in Manhattan, aren't familiar with Greenwich Village, and don't think it's a priority to live equidistant from a vintage clothing store, CVS, and 24-hour falafel stand, don't bother reading on. The significance of my day is in direct relation to the absurdity of my life, but absurdity is in the eye of the beholder, and my eye beholds Washington Square Park.

Some background:

I live in a rent-controlled apartment on a quiet-ish street in the heart of Greenwich Village. It's a two-bedroom, fourth floor walk-up in an old tenement building below an even older chess shop. The apartment consists of a small all-purpose room (approx. 200 sq. feet), a tiny bathroom (approx. shower stall-sized), and two bedrooms (I'm afraid to measure, but they fit beds, small dressers and armoires...because they don't have closets). By all-purpose room I mean kitchen, living room, dining room, library, solarium, office, and home gym. It's a Swiss Army room. For this château my roommate and I pay a very fair fee of $2,000 per month. To put it in perspective, my friend down the street pays $2,800 for the same sized space, and she doesn't have a bedroom window. Well, to put it in Manhattan-below-14th-street perspective.

Long story short:

My former roommate, an alcoholic yoga-freak who's since moved to Switzerland, holds the lease on my apartment. I found her on Craigslist (of course) and bribed her to pick me as her roommate with chocolate and alcohol (of course). She has held the lease for five years, thus stabilizing the rent. Last May she moved to Europe but agreed to keep the apartment in case she moves back. I currently pay rent through her or I did until she decided not to come back. We now have to break her lease. As I previously understood the terms of rent stabilization, changing the name on the lease leaves the apartment open to being re-listed at market value. The leaseholder stabilizes the rent so new holder equals new rent plus the standard down payment of two months rent.

One sentence synopsis: I was screwed.

The fear with which I went into that lease office to discuss the situation and find out just how expensive the apartment would now be cannot be described. If you've ever either searched for a Manhattan apartment or been beaten within inches of your life, you understand. Add to that the fact that my lease is up May 1st – day five of the Tribeca Film Festival, the thirteen day long marathon where I currently work. Also, I don't have enough savings for a realtor and can't technically pay market value for anything south of 125th Street. Things I was considering offering the landlord by way of begging for just one extra month in the apartment include: all of my shoes, the profits from my first book deal, or one to three of my eggs (as in the ones in my body).

I'm not sure what my stance is on God, miracles, luck, or Karma but I got whatever good there is to get by whatever or whoever is in charge of giving it. The apartment is rent-controlled, not rent-stabilized. In other words, I pay a security deposit and that's it. I have the option to auto-renew after six months with an increase of $50 to the total rent – fifty dollars. That's like one complete outfit from Forever21 per month! Even I can handle that. Oh, and there's a new Mexican restaurant opening two doors down.

The way we prioritize things in our early 20's is funny, I thought, after buying a celebratory bottle of wine that I will drink on my two-foot-long couch while cooking dinner with my left foot and doing leg curls with my right. Most people probably think I'm psychotic for being so ecstatic about holding on to my sad excuse for an adult apartment, which, though cheap for Manhattan, is *astronomical* for the world. They're probably right, but it's way too late now. I drank the Cool-aid and washed it down with a freshly fried Falafel. Now it's street chess with homeless dudes, tanning on the West Side Highway, and coffee shops with a wait-list until someone pries me from this heaven-sent apartment -- or I require a full-sized bed.

Ed note: Not only did I maintain my residence at 217 Thompson Street, Apt 21 for three more years and two more roommates, but after leaving I bequeathed the apartment to my cousin Geanna who later passed it down to my little sister Dani. By the end of our family's seven year run the rent was $2,100 per month – only 100 more than it was when I arrived and at that point 1,000 less than the cheapest apartment in the neighborhood. Letting it go remains the biggest regret of my life, but I still can't believe I fit all of my shoes and my person in that place at the same time.

To Choose a Choice

from 3/25/08

I've decided there are too many ways one can live one's life - too many versions of career and lifestyle, non-traditional and traditional, close to home and world traveling and cause-focused and family centered and totally moral and complete whore. Just too many choices.

I started thinking about this the first day I couldn't finish a day's work and a blog post. By the sixth day I was convinced – life choices are limiting. It's an obvious fact, but frustrating none-the-less. It reminds me of that day our senior year of college when Carly realized she'd never be a Laker Girl. We were watching something on TV – presumably a Lakers game. The girls finished doing their half time thing and a wash of disappointment passed over Carly's face. "Wow," she said, "I guess I'll never be a Laker Girl. I guess I missed that chance, huh? I'll probably never be an Olympic gymnast either. Huh. Wow." It's not that she ever wanted to be a Laker Girl; it's just the realization that when you choose a road – less traveled or otherwise – you're headed indefinitely in that one direction, not the other.

I really started thinking about this because I have a job that requires a good deal of commitment. It's not a j-o-b job, it's an investment job - the kind of job that consumes your life but you do it because you A. believe in what it accomplishes B. believe in what in will help you accomplish C. believe it's really worth the money or D. (but this is rare) all of the above. Mine is A. and a little of B. but mostly A. right now because I have no idea what I'm actually trying to B. (Yes! Unintentional word play!). C, not so much.

When I think about what choices lead me to this 16-hour-a-day, "investment opportunity," I'm confused – not confused like I was blacked out when I made them, confused like they don't seem as deliberate as I envisioned my major life choices being.

I left my first job working in PR at TheKnot.com (a wedding website) because I was miserable working in PR and among weddings (but mostly the latter). I ended up in PR because I was miserable in living at my parent's house and assisting a fashion designer (but mostly the former). I didn't really have career goals in the traditional sense. I had career likes: to write, to work in a creative environment, to interact with interesting brands doing innovative things - loose career goals. I had fairly definitive life goals: to live in Manhattan, to work in media, to expertly run along cobble stone streets in heels, to attend events where martinis were free - tight though bizarre life goals. I wouldn't say I made choices willy-nilly, but I didn't exactly choose something off the high school guidance counselor pick list (for the record, the multiple choice test pegged me as a librarian – hysterical considering I cannot whisper and do not understand anything involving decibels).

But again, I started thinking about all of this because right now filmmakers, specifically for the Tribeca Film Festival, surround me. I'm spending my 16-hour-a-day days building an event that's primary purpose is to help people who've made a very specific choice realize the dream, which prompted that choice. They don't have j-o-b jobs either; they have passion work. They don't make films. They are filmmakers. Like artists and writers. I'm committed to my job because I want to succeed, do well, progress, and feel confident. They're committed to their work because they can envision no other way to lead the one life they've been given. They made a choice. I chose a few things that dropped me in this current place. Sure I'll eat PB&J for a month if it means living in this city and affording clothes from the vintage shop across the street. Yes, I sometimes miss friend's birthdays because I have to work so late. I sacrifice things for the choices I've made – choices that I'm glad I've made. But I'm not pursuing a passion. Every step I take is not toward the goal of getting my next film made. I'm guided by my passions, definitely, but I'm not pursuing one passion – one singular goal against which all decisions are evaluated. That's one very specific way to lead one's life.

I realized after all this thinking that I'm jealous of the filmmakers. They made a choice and now, that thing they believe in more than any other thing drives every choice they make. To me, that's one enviable way to live one's life.

Me, I'm still looking for my ultimate choice, if there even is one. But in the meantime I figure I may as well help them with theirs, while running down cobble stone streets in my heels – on the way to free martinis.

Ed Note: Somewhere over the course of writing this blog, I chose a choice too. You'll see it as you read on. It starts as thoughts then morphs into writing on the wall before finally becoming a leap that transitions into a reality. Today I'm living that choice. I am like those filmmakers who inspired me all these years ago. If you had asked me when I decided that living the kind of life I currently live was the goal, I wouldn't have been able to tell you. Then I re-read this post and see that it lies within this melodrama mixed with jealousy. Side note: always pay close attention when you feel yourself experience wild jealousy….

It's crazy to read this light bulb going off and remember how it became much more than just a spark. A lot can happen in six years. Far more than I would have guessed at 24. Next to "mind your jealous moments" that's the lesson here.

Well...we're GChatting...

from 7/16/08

The process used to be so straightforward.

First High School:
- Admit you like him/her (but not to the actual person)
- IM (from the time you finish dinner 'til the time you go to bed)
- Round a base, or two (pre car: in basement parties when the strobe light goes on, post car: in the car)
- "We're going Out" (requested and confirmed via Instant Messager, exhibited by girl wearing mall-purchased ghetto chain of boy...in New Jersey at least)
- More base-rounding (in tandem with celebration of every single month of the relationship with gas station flowers and mix CDs)

    Communication tools: Phone (likely your own house line at this point), cell phone (but not really until junior or senior year), IM (home computer only), and e-mail (not widely used in friend communication)

Then College:
- Rounding the bases (quickly and sometimes in reverse)
- Talking (but not about anything having to do with a relationship at all ever)
- Going out (separately, but purposefully to the same places)
- Fighting (via passive aggressive away messages and drunken, too-loud comments to friends at parties)
- Repeat from top (but this time with declaration of "no attachment")

    Communication tools: Cell phone (including texting as of my junior/senior year), IM + away message (on all day, every day), e-mail (generally reserved for fighting, not flirting), and Facebook (for a limited number of colleges, only senior year).

And now, The Rest of our Goddamn Lives: (unless you cheated and went to some form of grad school then the above continues for two to four more years during which I seriously recommend you lock it down).

As far as I can tell there are no rules, no real process, and no one thing people are most commonly doing so you can just follow that crowd (unless you're Jewish, then it's JDate, so just do that). And to make matters worse (or perhaps what made matters worse?) we now have at our disposal no less than a baker's dozen communication tools over which we can play this game that has no rules:

- GChat, Facebook (and now Facebook chat!), MySpace (for the next few months before everyone switches to Facebook), Match.com/JDate/etc., IM, SameTime (if you work at an accounting firm, I'm told), cell phones (used only for texting), work phone, personal email, work email, Linked In (for stalking, not communicating, yet...)

And so now, in place of any agreed-upon process, you hear the following:

- I don't know where it's really going. We've been playing a lot of Scrabulous
- How weird would it be if I just Gchatted her? I mean, her Gmail is on her Facebook so that must mean she wants it to be known, right?
- Yeah, we've been texting for a few months now.
- I gave him my card but there's no way he's going to email my work email, right?!

We were more organized about dating in high school. Now you have to figure out how to
establish communication in one of the above eight forms, some of which are viewed as legitimate, some of which are not by some

people in some groups at some times under some circumstances.

I'm not longing for the olden days of "he pinned me" and "Pop, can you drive us to the drive-in?" but when people (parents) say, "What's so hard about it? Just contact him!" we have every right to whine, "over what medium!?!"

As a liberal, I'm not fond of social rules, but this shit needs to be solved. We need to write dating communication rules, post them on Facebook, and not accept behavior that is out of line with them. Then everyone's intentions will always be clear, and we'll all be married by 32 (34 for men, 28 for Southerners). Who's with me??

Ed Note: I read this post and think, yes, that is all still true. Then I think, ugh dating was rough, and also, my poor little sisters...

But very shortly after those sympathetic thoughts I think, who cares? Who is wasting all their time trying to interpret the behavior of a guy who only communicates with you via a Facebook game? Who is afraid to Gchat someone that they really like?

The answer, of course, is everyone, but if I'm learning one thing about dating in my 20s it's that none of that crap matters. When you really like someone, you let it all go. All the rules fly out the window, and all the fears (should) fly out with those rules. I know that applied to my own romantic situation (and that seemed to work out nicely). I know it applied to the situations of so many of my friends who I spent hours debating 140 character texts from men whose names I now forget.

I know it's hard. I know it feels like there are a thousand mistakes to make when you're doing the dance or playing the game or whatever the kids call it these days. I'm saying, there will come a time when you look back on all of that and say, I could have watched all five season of The Wire multiple times with the hours I spent dwelling on confusing people and more confusing dating rules. Go watch The Wire. It's wonderful television. You might even learn something about dating through the storylines. But even if you don't, I promise it will be more worth your time than trying to decide if, "yo, you up?" means, "I want to be your boyfriend," or, "I want you in my bed."

My Stab At "The"/ "A" One

from 7/28/08

Written from the perspective of a single, 20-something girl who hasn't had a boyfriend in more years than she's willing to reveal.

1. You can leave her alone at a party filled with people she doesn't know, and she'll have friends when you come back.

- It's not just that you don't want someone hanging all over you. It's that you want someone who is socially comfortable, adaptable to new situations and has a personality that lends to making friends easily. This will also make you look very good.

2. She quickly learns all your friend's names and nicknames, but knows when to use the real names and when to use the 'nicks.

- Druckman is Druckman to everyone, but using the name Jamal in reference to Pete should be cleared by the boys of Alpha Theta Ward. Read: she cares enough to know, but knows enough to understand your territory and hers. Fine line, but one that, when crossed, will rub the entire friend group the wrong way.

3. She makes it through each day without uttering one of the following, to you: Ugh, I feel so fat today! Oh my god these jeans are sooo tight on me. I want to wear that dress but it makes me look pregnant.

- Self-deprecation should be reserved for poignant, well-timed humor and, when themed around how a girl feels about her body, her girlfriends. We all have fat days and ugly days, but only the strongest among us don't whine about them to elicit response-compliments. You're not after a girl who never has a bad body day. You're after a girl who doesn't constantly put you in the very awkward position of having to say, "aww, you don't look fat today, or any day, ever."

4. She knows that at-the-bar-for-your-buddy's-birthday or when-the-guys-are-over-watching-football is not the time to pick a fight, no matter how seemingly important it is at the moment.

- This one's two-fold. It shows she can respect you and the situation and has advanced-enough fighting skills to know that no good can come from addressing it in that moment. She can be forgiven if she is excessively drunk – we've all been there - but pouting in a corner does not count as not bringing it up.

5. She calls, leaves a message and then waits until you call her back (unless she very seriously suspects that you are dead).

- In more specific words, she does not stalker call you until you pick up. Sure if she doesn't hear from you for hours and hours she can give it another attempt, but if you're not available at 10:00AM you're probably still not available at 10:01AM. Also when you say, "I have to go right now," she understands it means you'll still be doing whatever made you have to go five minutes later. This needs no further explanation.

6. She doesn't have an entire set of friends that she secretly hates.

- Girls are notorious for bad-mouthing friends behind their backs, but there's a difference between sometimes judgmental and always two-faced. Watch out for those. They might secretly hate you too.

7. She can make a decision without calling home.

- *Should I go to Law School?* probably necessitates a chat with Mom and Dad, but whether or not to get a haircut this Saturday could likely be handled independently.

8. This conversation never happens:

You: Last night was great.
Her: Pffft. Glad it was good for one of us (rolls eyes, returns to Us Weekly)

- Passive aggressiveness and sex go together like Britney Spears and her kids. She should be able to address it when it's happening and talk about it if there's a problem without an insulting, non-direct tone.

9. She loves Tina Turner.

- Tina Turner is a very sexy woman. She is also an excellent dancer with a healthy body and strong, optimistic outlook on life. A girl who loves Tina Turner is surely great in bed, takes care of her body, is driven to succeed, and can dance like nobody is watching. Frankly, you can disregard the rest of the list. This says it all.

Ed Note: I stand by every suggestion in this post but would like to point out that at the time of writing Britney Spears was engaged in a downward spiral the likes of which we did not see again until Charlie Sheen circa 2012. I'm still not sure she's fit to raise those two kids, but I'm going to limit my judgment to outlining the kind of woman every man should be dating and leave Britney to tabloids.

jessie rosen

Parents Are People Too

from 8/4/08

Rumor has it that when I was two years old I asked my Mom if we could be best friends.

"I can't remember what we were doing," she says now, "We were either having a tea party or I was reading you a book or, you know, maybe you were in the bathtub." There's a chance it was all three; I was raised a multi-tasker.

Apparently I looked up at her with my black/brown eyes and nose too big for my face and said, "Mommy, let's be best friends?"

She said okay, which was nice because I couldn't offer much by the way of traditional best friendship. My clothes were too small for her to borrow, and I didn't have any nail polish colors that she didn't already own. I guess in theory she could have talked to me about boy troubles, but I wouldn't have understood, plus they would have been about my Dad. She said yes anyway, and then I closed the book, finished my tea and got out of the tub.

It dawned on me yesterday, two hours into a discussion about her most recent full body skin scan, that she'd taken me seriously. I'd asked if we could be best friends, she'd agreed, and now we were – in her eyes – best friends for life - names as good as written in Sharpie on the bathroom wall.

Do not get me wrong. Being so close to my mother is one of the things I'm most grateful for in my life (it goes Mom, rent-controlled apartment, skin that tans, and Downy Wrinkle Releaser, but sometimes apartment, Mom, Downy, skin depending on how much I've seen her lately and how quickly I need to change outfits). But if I'd known she'd hold me to my toddler request, I might have laid some best friendship ground rules - rules specific to the fact that she is my Mom. Like, mention of any and all thoughts regarding your marriage are off limits. I realize this is an important part of girl-talk but you're married to my Dad, sorry. I'll promise not to share things I've done between three and seven o'clock in the morning for the past five years in exchange. Also, conversations about how you want your funeral handled should be reserved for your lawyer and/or Dad. While I appreciate you wanting to work through the details with a listening ear, I generally try to avoid conversation about the saddest things that will ever happen to me. Things specific to your female aging body parts should also be kept to yourself. It's not that I'm unsympathetic or skeeved out, it's that I have half of your genes and don't particularly want a preview of what's to come.

Whether or not you and your parents exchanged neon friendship bracelets and BFF badges in Girl Scouts, the fact is that sometime over the past five years our parents became like this weird version of our peers. Long gone are the days of Mrs. Cunningham staying out of everyone's business and the stoic, one-beer-at-dinner dad from the *Wonder Years*. Our parents want to be involved in our lives and therefore, they assume, we should be involved in theirs – everything from the day-to-day, "Jim got the promotion I'd been gunning for so I'm having a rough day," to the more broadly themed, "You just cannot imagine the devastation of caring for your grandmother like she is a child."

Apparently parents are people too - people who now view us as capable of hearing their issues and providing the kind of comfort and support they've provided us for the past 20-some years. Unfortunately, I can't handle it.

It's somewhat like seeing the middle school teacher you adore buying hemorrhoid crème at the local CVS. You get that teachers don't live at the school and are probably married, but in your eyes the universe simply protects them from hemorrhoids and all other negatives because they are your favorite teacher. That same thing applies to parents.

You don't want to deny them a real life filled with real feelings - pain included - but you need to go on believing they are invincible heroes with emotions of steel and no financial issues. Their regular sharing of feelings is really inconvenient to your plan of never having to acknowledge that they are human.

It's funny. I can sit with a friend who's just been dumped for hours as she sobs about how torn apart she is. I've even been there for a friend who's experienced the death of a parent and provided support without completely losing it. But the minute my Mom launches into a, "your Father really hurt my feelings the other day," I want to curl up into a ball and die. Instead I usually yell, "AAHHH GOD STOP!" before she can get to whatever it is that she needs to get off her chest. Mature, I know.

It happened again this past weekend. She was going on comparing her marriage to that of her friends and *blah blah*. I was singing Rihanna's "Disturbia" over and over in my head because I know all the words and like to keep segments of time as well-themed as possible.

"Are you listening to me?" she said ten to fifteen minutes in. We were alone on the beach. Now was my chance. I'd planned this speech a thousand times in my head.

"Mom, I love you very much, and I can never thank you enough for the years of support and counsel you've given me. You have made me the person I am today. That said, I find it unbearable to hear you talk about issues involving your deepest feelings because it affects my deepest feelings, and thus I find myself sad/stressed/worried about/for you. I would prefer to go on believing you are unaffected by the troubles of the world. This is not fair, mature or at all in keeping with my former request to be your best friend. Therefore I'm afraid I have to retract that request and ask that we, instead, move to becoming really good friends who talk endlessly about a to-be-determined list of items. How does that sound?"

Impressive, right? Too bad that instead I say this: "Sorry, I was just distracted by that guy over there. What were you saying?"

The woman once took three, back-to-back, incoherent 2:00AM calls from me after someone went home with someone who was not me. She then stayed up for an additional hour to write me a loving email about the maturity level of most guys and the simple facts about binge drinking. Also when I was broken in Florence she wired me $500 and handled telling my Dad.

If anything, she should retract the best friendship. Instead, I'll just grow a set.

Ed Note: My mother continues to share feelings that I'd prefer to believe do not exist, but now that my sisters are both older and in closer proximity, they handle a fair share of the daughter-therapy. That said, every so often as I'm sitting on a beach, watching TV on the couch, or walking through a mall I wish my Mom was right there by my side, telling me about the giant mole she just had removed on her back.

What's Your Scary Age?

from 8/7/08

I think it was Katie who coined the term "scary age" – as in, "26 is my scary age." It must have been sometime directly after graduation when we took to assigning maxims to everything about post-grad life. Like, "I'll know it's really over when I can't go out three nights in a row," (check) or, "the first time I mistakenly make-out with someone who's still in college, I'm going to lose it," (double check). The scary age thing fit in among those conversations, aka *all* conversations. I've always hated the concept but probably because it - like that damn biological clock - is a reality.

Scary age is hard to pin point. Says Katie, "it's the point at which I feel like I really have to get my life together - like every decision from here on out has to be really deliberate towards some kind of end life happiness." Says Nora, "25."

To me, it's like from zero to scary age is all that stuff in your *E! True Hollywood Story* that comes before the deep, scary-man voiceover says, "and *then*...just after her 20-something-th birthday...it all _____ (came together/fell apart/made sense/came out of the closet)." Your goal is to make it so there's light and happy, not dark and terrifying music in the background – color pictures of you holding awards and not black and whites of you holding empty bottles.

Broad terms – our scary age is the year we freak out over where we've been, where we're going, and how it rates. In our minds we want all the pieces of our *Sim Life* lined up and ready to go by X date of X year – certain things should be built, other things should be in queue for building, and everything else should be sitting in our *Sim Life* dashboard, awaiting proper placement on the grid. 25, 26, 27, 28 – doesn't matter. We lock it in and there it sits, waiting to arrive like some whole-life SAT except you write all the questions *and* all the answers and somehow still don't think you'll get one right. The markers you hit or miss are part your own invention, part societal pressure. It's *your* goal to be published by 29. It's *society's* fault that most people are married by 27. The details don't matter. It's that unfortunate fact that you only live once, and by X age you want to feel like you're doing it right.

I don't know if there's a correlation between someone's scary-age and their general personality. I'd think the more focused, the least scared, but it could be that focus leads to goals, which lead to failures and thus freak-outs? Maybe it's the less directed, the more adaptable, so the less consumed with benchmarks, and thus the better off? I'm told there are people who really do believe age is just a number, but I've decided not to believe they exist because it makes me feel better about myself. I admit that I've yet to hear a male use the term scary age, but maybe that's just because like *that's such a nightmare* or *I'm in a funk* just doesn't come out of (straight) male mouths.

Over-dramatics aside (for this paragraph), life stages are marked by numbers. At those numbers we hope to hit goals, make progress, and feel *correct* in this world – like our life has a thesis statement, and we're following it.

Today I turned some people's scary age (some people being Katie) - 25. I'm a quarter of a century, half way to 50, closer *to* 40 than from it, and an official renter of cars.

I'm safe because it's not my scary age. Mine was 26, but now it's 27 on account of inflation and my dating record.

25, though, still holds a certain weight in my head, though, like this marker of actual adulthood signifying the end of getting away with blatant immaturity (in public). I feel like at 25 I have to sit myself down and say, "Okay, where are we are? Oats, sewn; money, squandered; gateway drugs, tried; slippery slope through gateway, avoided; and metaphoric notches in (twin) bedposts, carved. Good work, now stop blacking out and start saving money."

It's like from here on out I don't have to move forward in one, focused direction, but I can't blatantly move backward. I've made some solid ground and lived a life of which 80% could be shared with my parents; now my life's purpose is to not F it up. 25, the year I do as I say and not as I want?

For now, I'm two years from "scary" and feeling like I've finally arrived at the age I've been dressing for since pre-school. Who knows, maybe by the time I approach my scary age inflation will push it from 28 to 30. Or maybe I'll just actually accomplish all I've hoped for and be fully set on everything else I want exactly three years from this day. Wish me luck.

Ed Note: I invited Katie to reflect on this post because she started the whole "scary age" thing in the first place. Kate, take it away.

From my perch here at 30, reflecting on this blog post and on my twenties overall, I am absolutely blown away to think of all the things I would have missed if I had "settled down" by 25. Between 25 and 30 I quit my unfulfilling job, took out scary-big loans, became a full time student again, traveled to 13 new countries, worked on an AIDS project in Africa, saw three Wonders of the World, moved to a city I would have <u>never</u> imagined I would want to live in, am on a career path to a dream job that I literally did not know existed when I was 25, made amazing friends in two new cities, and have met the love of my life. Not a bad five years! And really, really important years... Full of adventures and self-discovery and relationship building and soul-searching. If I had stopped that personal development process at 25 to "get my life together", I would have missed so, so many things that I didn't yet realize would make my life amazing. Scary.

jessie rosen

You Know You're Not in College Anymore When...

from 9/8/08

It's hard to wrap your brain around how not in college you are until you pay a visit to your alma mater and hang out with your sisters who now both go there, for example...

Me: So do you think everyone thinks I'm a student?
Sara: No, you look old.

Every moment is a reminder of the fact that your chapter ended 3 + years ago and now someone else is having the best time of your life, only better.

Me: My god that little girl has a blackberry!
Some kid: Everyone has a blackberry. Where have you been?

In hell, kid. I've been in hell.

There's no lack of striking juxtapositions between college life and now, but over the course of my three days at Boston College Parents Weekend (during which I was neither a student nor a parent), none was more depressing than watching my sister and her five best friends get ready for a party in their Mod (a 1,500 square foot, two story condo equipped with 2.5 bathrooms, free furniture, and a backyard located among 65 other Mods in a section of senior housing best compared to heaven). In general, I avoid being a Debbie Downer, but this shit was too upsetting to endure alone:

Getting dressed

- Senior Year of college: Depending on friend's clothing sizes, you have between three and six full wardrobes to select from. My sister's Mod is complete with five full length mirrors in addition to five best friend fashion consultants who will go so far as to select a complete ensemble for you if you don't feel like it slash are already too drunk. They will also do your hair and/or make-up.

  Junior Year of the-rest-of-your-life: Depending on the size of your apartment, you have between .5 and .75 wardrobes to select from. There's a 30% chance you have a full-length mirror and a 20% chance your roommate is home to dress you – though even if she was it's now too weird to ask because you met her on Craigslist.

Pre-gaming

- 21: Power Hour around 9PM to kick off the evening. Best option for a five to seven hour evening with a peak around 2AM. This has been tested at length.

  25: 10:30PM, half-dressed, alone in your room listening to your power hour soundtrack from college. Your in-house options are a glass of wine or a beer. Go wine and you might fall asleep before midnight, again. Go beers and you might not fit into your outfit within the hour.

Boys

- College: You know exactly who's coming, approximately who you will make out with and are in discussion with the girls around the short list of B-list boys should the need arise.

  NYC: You assess chances of meeting a straight, decent guy around 10%. Chances of seeing said straight, decent guy after hypothetical meeting, 3%.

The Scene

- Time of your life: Your entire extended friend group in your living room drinking 30's of Busch Lite that cost $14.99 a piece to a mix of music you spent your entire summer perfecting.

    Now: Let's just leave it at two drinks cost more than that whole 30 pack, and your entire friend group hasn't been in the same place in three years.

I got more than one weird look as I screamed, "SAVOR EVERY MOMENT!!" upon leaving my sister's Mod. Then I saw a guy projectile vomit onto the girl holding him up outside my sister's place. "Eeeww! I am totally not hooking up with you tonight now!" she said.

Hm. Right, I thought. Do not miss that.

Ed Note: I want to say something about life getting really fun and exciting once you're finally settled into your 20s, and that is true, but what's more true is that there is NO time like college, and I miss my best girlfriends almost every single time I get dressed to go out. Thank god for weddings…

Also, sorry to be a Debbie Downer. I promise it only happens when college vs. real life is involved.

Go to a Bar Alone

from 8/23/08

I told myself I wasn't going to go there – there being here – but the conversation has come up too many times to ignore. So by popular request, I am ashamed to introduce the most lame and clichéd series to hit this or any blog:

How Slash Where to Meet People to Date Slash Marry

(somewhat proven advice that's not sure-fire or necessarily safe)

1. Go to a bar alone.

In other words – intentionally go without any other people to a place that serves alcohol and enjoy drinks sans the planned company of others. Sorry. The first time I told someone to do this they said, "what do you mean?!"

Here's how and why it works:

How It Works

- Pick a spot with a long bar you know will be fairly crowded with the type of people you like at a reasonable hour on a weeknight that people go out. I'd do Barrow Street Ale House in Manhattan's West Village. Thursday. 7pm. You get an after happy hour crowd of people still drinking but not black out. So, the fun ones.

- Sit at the bar and order something respectable (read: not pink). Tip the bar tender well. If the first person who sidles up is a douche, you want the 'tender in your corner. It can also pay off to strike up a convo with him/her. Could turn into group talk with the bar sitters. Huge move.

- Engage in some form of banal activity that prompts curiosity but not intimidation. I'd go pages of whatever writing I'm working on and a little notebook. I'm casually reading and jotting things down while maintaining a look of coy openness to the question, "what's that you're working on?" Other options: weekly news magazine, movie script (www.imsdb.com), book with lots of pictures. Not options: Sudoku, your phone, nail polish.

- Set a time or drink limit and do not move. Your mantra: this is not weird. Think of the bar as a much-more-fun coffee shop. You would have no problem at all sitting alone at a Starbucks sipping coffee and reading the paper (if you would, get over it). The bar is like Starbucks but people get drunk, feel bold, and talk to each other. It does not matter why you are there alone, but if someone wants to know what your story is, they can ask. Mission accomplished.

Why It Works

- You and your four best friends dressed up on a Friday night in a crowded, sweaty bar filled with a dime-a-dozen groups just like you is just bad odds. Dating is a numbers game. Put them in your favor.

- While this is not weird (keep saying it) people don't traditionally do it meaning when they do, it's noted and interesting to people who respect confident, interesting people. These are the people you want to meet slash be.

- What do you have to lose? The answer is: the cost of one to three beers, pride if you happen to run into an ex and time if it doesn't work out. But remember, bars aren't just filled with people who might have date offers. They also feature people who offer jobs, apartments, or good advice. Hardly a waste.

Yes I realize this seems contrived. That's because it is. There are lots of less contrived ways to meet people if you'd prefer. Popular examples include staring them down from across a party, winking at them from match.com, and telling your friends you really, *really* want to meet them, but you're probably already doing all of those...

Ed Note: In the six year history of 20-Nothings.com THIS is the most read entry. It turns out people organically search "go to bar alone" on Google a TON, and apparently this is one of the only articles out there on the topic. To me, this means two things. 1. People are way too addicted to Google and 2. Nobody knows how to do anything alone anymore. I am happy to have done what little I could do to solve issue number two. Regarding the first problem, I've used it to my advantage by writing an article called "How To Ask Someone Out" and "How To Dump Someone." If you can't beat 'em, use 'em!

I Grew Up A Little Bit on Sunday at 8:30PM

from 10/13/08

You know you've grown up a little bit when you can look back on your previous self and make that sound my Mom makes when they won't apply a coupon to sale merchandise – total disgust.

Around 8:30PM today I reflected on my 3:45PM self and made that exact sound.

Michael and I had spent the day engaged in one of our favorite Manhattan activities: walk around the city and try to find things you've never seen before (working title). This time we found an 18th century Chinese village and the NYC jail – a series of building that look like Soviet Russia. It was a striking juxtaposition.

Near the end of our walk Michael noticed the newly opened store of

Designer Billy Reid – a recent recipient of the CFDA award for new male designer. If you know what that means, awesome!! right?! If you don't - Michael saw a cool new store.

The store was like if EPCOT created a nation of pristine 1950s Charleston South Carolina - immaculate details of re-created vintage in an old building on the newly reclaimed Bowery. If you are the kind of person deeply affected by environment, this was a place you'd overhaul your entire wardrobe and then potentially change your name for (I'm between Delilah and Amelia. Thoughts?).

Naturally I found a dress. Well I found eight dresses and tried on six, but one was the one. I admittedly have an unhealthy attachment to clothing, so to best understand this story please replace "a dress" with whatever thing you cannot resist. If you can't think of such item, you can stop reading this post and probably the blog in its entirety. You are an adult.

Now in general, I can resist an expensive dress, but with this dress I also found a man named Jeremy, designer Billy Reid's partner. Michael and I remain unclear on the meaning of partner in this context. He referenced building a lot of things (straight) but also styling a lot of things (gay), offered us an alcoholic drink (just plain smart) and touched my butt a few times as I was trying on the dresses (welcome, but confusing). Either way it didn't matter. He loved the dress and I loved him. Sold.

At $295 it was well beyond my price range (which for reference is free to $39.99). The only things I've purchased near that amount in recent history are a plane ticket to L.A. and three months of backed-up electric bills.

No matter. Jeremy was having it shipped from Florence, Alabama where it is hand made in my smaller size. I'd just go on the Special K diet (just two bowls a day and a healthy third meal!) until the dress arrived jointly saving money and maintaining my smaller size.

The list of places I would wear this new dress were endless - on a date with a Lower East Side musician, to an art gallery crawl in Williamsburg, to a party in a West Village townhouse thrown by the editor of nymag.com. I would need brown, lace-up boots and chestnut highlights, but it would be spectacular.

I was planning all such occasions later that evening during the previews for Rachel Got Married (didn't love it, but Debra Winger is great). I don't know how or why it happened, but I envisioned going to pick the dress up and paying for it with my credit card when that total disgust sound came out of my mouth.

You have zero need for that dress – my sound mind said. You

can't afford it. Also you never met anyone who lives on the LES, don't know where Williamsburg is, and in no way belong at the editors party. Grow up. And with that, the shoulder-perched angel got one victory over the better-dressed-but-totally-broke devil, and I grew up a little.

I'll probably go back for one last look at my almost mistake. I might even try it on again while enjoying a little bourbon and a lot of Jeremy, but I will not buy. This one Sunday afternoon in 2004 I grew up from turning back from previously sworn against mistakes. Hhmm. Must be a Sunday thing.

Ed Note: I know you're going to cry bullshit on this, but in the almost five years since writing this post, I have yet to spend $295 dollars on a dress, or any other single clothing item for that matter. I don't even think I've spent $200. There was a time after that one shopping experience that I finally became able to afford dresses around that price range, but it somehow seemed silly to blow all that newly earned money on one item versus the entire wardrobe I could buy at H&M. Plus, you can find killer discounts at your local Marshalls, T.J. Maxx and Nordstrom Rack. And so I am proud to say that I have maintained that level of adult behavior since it first arrived. That said, I am in no way closer to being able to drink alcohol and not eat whatever cheese is in sight.

A Modern Meet Cute Theory

from 10/28/08

I'm not saying it's a hard and fast rule, but I do believe the weirder the places you put yourself in the greater your chances are of meeting someone – case in point the guy I met at a hot dog stand at three o'clock in the morning.

I had been out with some friends on the Lower East Side – Libation I think? – for one or too many vodka tonics, my drink of choice at the time. I've since switched to vodka, soda on account of the popularity of skinny jeans. I had to go to the bathroom because I have the bladder of an eight-month pregnant woman, so I went wandering around downstairs looking for the loo. I eventually found it behind a red velvet curtain (typical), went, and then somehow walked out the front door of the bar. I have no idea how this happened. I can assume from my state of mind (or lack there of) that I thought the front door was the stairs back to the dance floor. This has happened before.

Once on the street I decided I might as well go home. Again, these are assumptions. It is entirely possible that I had another destination in mind. No matter because on the way to wherever I was headed, I smelled hot dogs.

I, like most people who claim to be grossed-out by hot dogs, love them. I take mine with sauerkraut and brown mustard, exclusively. Of course, drunk at 3:00AM, I'd take it any way it was offered.

And so I proceeded to sniff around the dark and unsavory streets of the Lower East Side looking for the source of this hot dogs smell. I'm sorry Mom. Really I am.

Luckily the source was actual hot dogs. I found them somewhere shockingly far from where I began (apparently when the sense of logic is dulled, the sense of smell is sharpened?). Now at this far away hot dog cart stood a very attractive man. I must have approached looking like a McGruff on a mission, because he said something like, "wow, you look like you really want a hot dog! Let me buy that for you." That or I looked amazing and he had an extra $1.50 burning a whole in his pocket.

This is where my theory comes in. See if I had simply been in a subway car with this guy…or inside a store…or sitting on a park bench, he would have had no natural prompt to start a conversation. It was because I was a laughable disaster in an already hysterical environment that he had an opening line -- a meet-cute as the 1940's filmmakers would call it.

They didn't have sauerkraut, but I wasn't about to refuse a free hot dog from a perfectly good-looking man. I believe we stood there for some time as the vendor (a man whose version of this story I would kill to hear) prepped the dog because we somehow grew comfortable enough with each other for him to ask for my number and kiss me. Yes, hot dog in left hand, high-heeled foot dangling off the cracked, concrete curb, I kissed a boy at a late night food cart.

But again, it was because of the very bizarreness of the situation that the chain of events occurred. I've had similar luck standing and watching the trapeze school that used to be outside Hudson River Park ("so, are you a trapeze artist or just a fan?") and at the New York City Transit Museum ("so, what's your favorite subway line?") leading me to believe that the stranger the circumstance, the more natural the conversation.

And no, my hot dog man never called. Apparently you've got to kiss a lot of guys at hot dog stands at 3:00AM to get a prince?

Ed Note: A few months after this I met and started dating a man who I cast as a character in my one-act play. Before our short-lived relationship, I would have said that our meeting only further proved my "meet cute" theory. It is completely bizarre to meet a man auditioning to play a character you created, thus you are more likely to strike up a conversation around similar interests and maybe, ultimately, date. After our short-lived relationship I would say that there are certain specific places that you should consider off limits for meeting men. For me that is a list of one, and it is "casting sessions for anything you've written."

My 80-Year-Old Dentist on Online Dating

from 1/30/09

On Wednesday night I went to the dentist. Since graduation from my parent's insurance I haven't had dental insurance because all small communication companies ironically view it as an *option* to have a healthy mouth.

Now at job number three I have secured dental insurance so I can finally go find out that I have seven cavities and inoperable gum disease. This is my uneducated assumption because sometimes my molars hurt, and on occasion I do see a little pink in the sink.

I go to the first dentist I can find in network that has availability within the month and is located near a subway stop. This, in hindsight, is more like the way one should go about finding a $60, 50 minute Chinese massage, not professional mouth care involving sharp tools.

My new dentist, Docta' *Saaands* as he was exclusively called by his secretary, is located on the 4th floor of a non-descript building in a neighborhood I didn't previously know existed. "We're in the *gova*'ment ney-ba' hood," she told me on the phone.

"You mean the *Financial* District?" I said.

"No, I mean what just came outta my mouth! *Gov a' ment*!"

I should have cancelled, but I really was worried about that pink in the sink.

Docta' Sands office was like Willy Wonka's office in the end of the movie (Gene Wilder version, *of course*) when Charlie and Grandpa go try to apologize for stealing the

EverLastingGobstopper, except instead of everything being half *there* everything was just half dirty. Docta Sands, however, appeared to be fully *clean* but only half there.

"How are we all today?" he said to a completely empty waiting room and me. "Good to hear," he said before I responded. "Ga' head and pick a chair ova' where the dentist chairs are. I'll see ya' in a little bit."

This is when I take out my Moleskin. If this is going to be painful, I better at least get a story out of it.

I pick the chair closest to the door.

In, oh, ten maybe *twelve excruciating minutes,* he saunters in. He appears to have just taken the final bite of a large roast beef sandwich with sauerkraut. To give you a visual, he is George Costanza's father except six feet tall and as tan as Fabio. I envision a half dirty house in Boca…

Then, without hesitation, reference to my teeth, or the application of one of those spittle bibs, he launches into this:

- DRS: So – ya' married?
- Me: Nope
- DRS: Ya' wanna be?
- Me: Eventually.
- DRS: I don't think ya' wanna be.
- Mo: Excuse me?
- DRS: Ya very non-chalant about it. (At this point he's started taking out the various pointy dental tools and arranging them on the tray.)
- Me: No, no, sorry. I would like someday to be married, but I don't have a boyfriend right now.
- DRS: Interesting. (He literally looks me up and down, which is awkward because I am laying horizontal.)
- Me: Why…do you know someone? (Two can play at this game.)

- DRS: Sure. How 'bout Miguel in the chair over there? (He points to the *extremely* not sound-proof half-wall separating me from, apparently, Miguel)
- Me: Sshhh! He can hear you!
- DRS: What? You like 'um deaf? (I laugh then think, *shit*. I've encouraged him.)
- DRS: Well listen. I tell ya' what - I do know some people, but I think you gotta go online first.
- Me: Excuse me?
- DRS: You on Craigslist?
- Me: *Craigslist?* I'm not sure that's a real dating site.
- DRS: Sure it is, and a free one ta' boot!
- Me: Ok, well, I'm not really interested in that path.
- DRS: You wanna; know what's wrong with you people?
- Me: What people?
- DRS: You young women people.
- Me: Oh. (Here we go....)
- DRS: You're all just too all ova' the place with ya' profiles about ya'selves. Always I love to bicycle and read mystery novels and go to the beach and eat the sushi and work out three days a' the week and small dogs and yadda yadda. It's too much! (He throws one of the small pointy instruments on the floor in exclamation. I decide firmly that if he picks it up and tries to use it again in my mouth, I will leave)
- DRS: I tell ya' what ya' needa' do. You needa' say, 'Sometimes I like ta stay home and relax…sometimes I like ta' party. You take me out, you find out more.' And that's it! Done!
- Me: Well I don't know…
- DRS: Nope! That's it! Ya' done! (Now he is flailing the electric toothbrush around, wizzing flecks of that fake toothpaste all over the room as he makes his grand point)
- Me: Okay. (It is not worth arguing with this man)
- DRS: So – ya' set. You let me know how that works out for ya' okay? Now, do ya' floss? Neva' mind, ya' don't floss. I can see *that* plain as day.

And there you have it. Words of wisdom from an 80-some-year-old man who appears to have spent some time trolling the Craigslist want adds.

Maybe he's right. Maybe that approach really is the way to hook a guy online. Unfortunately I won't be finding out or reporting back. According to Docta Sands I have no cavities and there's nothin' wrong with a little pink in the sink. Next month I'll be seeking a second opinion on the Upper East Side. I bet they don't even know Craiglist exists up there.

Ed Note: I never saw Docta' Sands again, but soon after I moved to L.A. where another dentist told me that I had eight cavities and needed to convert to Judaism to meet a man. See page 158 for that story.

Adopt-A-Boyfriend

from 2/11/09

I recently started sponsoring a child in El Salvador because the guy selling sponsorships was really attractive.

I believe this is what they're referring to when they reference, "rock bottom."

It was a cold and snowy afternoon in Manhattan, and I was coming home from seeing *The Wrestler* and grabbing a sandwich at Tiny's Giant Sandwich shop with my friend Chris. Justin *Hi-I'm-a-Mac* Long was there, as was a guy who may or may not have been Colin Hanks. For the purposes of this story, let's say it was.

Afterwards I strolled home in the beautifully falling snow reflecting on how much I love Manhattan and whether or not I should stop at Urban Outfitters to see if those knee-high grey suede boots got any cheaper.

I was so distracted that I missed the street hawking "Save the Children" volunteers corralling people as they moseyed down Broadway.

These guys are rogue marketing geniuses. Instead of, "Excuse me, do you have a few minutes for starving children in Africa?" it's now, "Hey! Do you hate babies?!" to which you have to say "no" because only an asshole hates babies...openly.

I looked up from my boot-dreaming stupor to see a very attractive brown-haired man (you can't call a man a brunette) standing directly in front of me - arms spread wide, big attractive grin on his three-day-beard face (S: scruff is among my deal *enhancers* which are not the same as deal *makers* and obviously the opposite of deal-*breakers*).

"Hey! How much do you love your Mom?!" he said. I mean...

"A lot," I said, "she's great."

"You probably love her because she gave you so much love and attention when you were growing up, right?" he said.

"Yes, that's among the reasons," I said. *"Would you call your eyes ocean blue or sky blue?"* I thought.

Now typically I would have seen this guy from 30 yards away, pulled out my cell phone and engaged in the following fake conversation:

"Listen, I know we don't really have the funds, but these are *disabled children* we're talking about. I want you to go find the money and don't call me back until you've got it, ya' hear?!" This varies depending on the agency I'm ignoring.

But typically this street hawker would be 18-years-old and a girl. Not the case here. Not at all.

It pains me to say that I legitimately believed there was a chance something might develop between this man who gets money for potentially fake children on the streets of Manhattan, but I did, fully.

"I'm sure she is great. I mean look at *you*," he said. My F enhancer is forward flattery...

I blushed under the hood of my parka.

"So listen," he leveled with me, "you know the drill here. I'm outside in the cold trying to help some kids by asking people for a low monthly fee of $22. That's two cocktails a month. Do you drink two cocktails a month?"

No, beautiful man, I drink 30, but for you I could cut it down to 28...

"Ha, clever, I like your style," I said. I claim to be many things, not-obvious is not one of them.

"Well I like that you like it," he said with his Josh Hartnett-hot grin. If I were watching this interaction from above I would have slapped me and told him he should be ashamed of himself. Instead I said," You know, I *am* doing a few more freelancing writing assignments this month *so*..."

"Oh you're a *writer*?" he said. Mission accomplished.

"Gosh, I don't know if I'd call myself a *writer*, but I just love to write so I do as much as I can, ya know? It's really competitive in the city, so I'm lucky to get any work really..."

I should have just said that I don't love my Mom, that would have made me less of an asshole than I was currently being.

"That's really impressive," he said, "It sounds like you understand what it's like to struggle." ...Like a starving child in El Salvador, was what he seemed to strangely imply.

"Yes, totally," I said. ...I am going to buy this child from you because you're very attractive, is what I'm sure my very obvious implication made clear.

Fifteen minutes later, I was the proud benefactor of a 6-year-old boy named Frank who lives in a South American city that would *destroy* my chances at winning *Where in the World is Carmen Sandiego*. I would 100% run to the wrong side of the giant floor map pissing off all the smarter, foreign kids watching at home. "Ugh over *there*!!! You idiot! Go left...*LEFT*! It's in *ASIA!!* Ugh, dumb Americans..."

At several points in our "conversation" I considered nudging it to the next level. "So does your girlfriend do this sort of work too…?" but my right mind won out.

Dave - that was his name - said I could cancel my donation within 30 days if I found I couldn't manage the commitment, but I've decided that if I'm dumb enough to sponsor the kid for the most cliché reason in the book then I deserve at least one year of $22 monthly fees.

Plus, there's still that chance he'll go back to search my donor profile so he can grab my email address to follow up and ask me out, and I can't have him see that I've cancelled my donation and decide I'm not the honest, starving-children-loving girl he was looking for, now can I?

Ed Note: To this day, almost six years later, I still contribute $22 per month to Frank, my sponsor child in El Salvador. Dave never e-mailed and is now likely married with at least one kid, and yet we still share that special moment on a snowy day in Manhattan – a moment he likely never thought of again. I, on the other hand, think of it every single month as I pay the $22 from my bank account and considering canceling the donation…

When it Becomes Riskier to Not Go After the Girl

from 5/20/09

My friend John recently confirmed my long-held belief that when a guy's ready, nothing will stop him from pursuing a girl.

John's a catch. He's a musically-talented, Boston College-educated, 4th year med student with a great sense of humor and a group of guy friends that people write TV shows and movies about (not literally, yet...). As such, he has dated his share of quality ladies - some for legitimate amounts of time. But when each relationship ended, John would admit that he just wasn't ready to get in that kind of committed situation.

> "Then you must not like her that much..." I'd argue.

> "I don't know," he'd say, "I'm just not ready yet."

Classic guy line.

But suddenly, this past weekend, over one of our tri-monthly check-ins (if that means every 3rd month?) he sang a very different tune.

"Jessie," he said, "I think I'm at that point where I could really date a girl for awhile now -- really be in a relationship." And then he shared the following story, which I hope I'm not butchering...

John is a runner so he went into a running store to buy whatever it is they sell there (I've never been). At said store was a shop girl he found instantly attractive. She may or may not have been related to the storeowner? I can't remember. Given the logistics of John's shopping transaction, there wasn't occasion to ask for her number (note that he never mentioned just leaving his number behind. He wanted *hers*.), so he went back a few days later to see if she was there intending to fake buy, I don't know, probably socks (running includes socks, right?).

Sadly there was no shop girl that day, but John wasn't about to let this die. He sought the help of a doctor who works in his hospital and also frequents this local running shop (what is *everyone* a runner?). He hoped the doctor might also remember this girl and might have a relationship with the storeowner, being a frequent customer. John was right. The doctor referred him to a family friend of the storeowner who, through two additional steps that were a bit unclear (John mumbles sometimes), procured the girl's cell phone number. John called it the day he got it and left a message for the girl.

This specific story is open-ended because shop girl's on vacation for the rest of this week, but that's not the point.

The point is that John finally arrived at a place where he viewed it as riskier to *not* go to those lengths to get the girl. "I'm just at this point where I don't care anymore," he told me, "I'm going to pursue it if I think there's something there." Is it one parts balls, one part logic and the rest what my Mom would call, "a feeling?" I don't know, and I don't know if John really knows either.

There's this Anaïs Nin quote I've always really loved that goes, "And the day came when the risk to remain tight in a bud was more painful than the risk it took to blossom."

That is hokey, and John will roll his eyes when he reads it, but that's exactly his situation. It wasn't about this specific girl -- he 100% doesn't know her. It's about him being in a place where any girl of remotely strong interest is worth pursuing because he's ready to find someone great. Maybe she'll blow him off. Maybe she'll be the greatest girl he's ever met. The point is that he'll now take the embarrassment of the blow off in exchange for her maybe being the greatest.

The question -- per usual -- is why. What changed in his outlook?

When did it start? And will he revert back if a few pursuits don't work out?

We'll see what he has to say after I tell him I wrote this post about his story and now need answers.

Ed Note: I wasn't able to get a comment from John because it's very busy being a full-blown doctor these days, but I imagine he would say he stands by everything above.

For my own, personal connection to this now-proven theory, you'll have to read through to page 137. No cheating.

Aluminum Magnolias

from 6/22/09

There are things you know you'll have to start dealing with once you're well into your 20's: get job, keep job, progress at job; get apartment, pay rent on apartment, don't burn down apartment; find significant other, keep significant other, don't cheat on significant other. They're right-of-passage-things that, when you do them right, make you feel okay in the world, like you might actually have this whole be-an-adult thing under control.

Then there are things that happen once you're well into your 20's that you forgot you'd have to deal with -- things you haven't particularly prepared for -- things that sort of happen *upon* you, and suddenly you find yourself in them, and because you're in them as a person well into your 20's, you have to deal with them like a legitimate adult should – no temper tantrums, no selfish running away, no shoving things off on other people that are technically your job.

Losing your first grandparent is one of these things. It arrives around this age for many of us because of typical life timelines, but isn't something we account for in the mix of "things that happen at this age." Once age 22 hit I didn't start investing in my 401K, taking a daily women's vitamin, and preparing for the death of my Mommom. I haven't practiced the wake and funeral process like I have cooking Thanksgiving dinner. I never sat my little sisters down and said, "Okay when this happens I'll play the role of X if you guys handle Y, Z, and ZZ," (there are four of us).

And so here I am with a chunk of money saved, fairly healthy bones, a solid command of the cooking of a turkey and absolutely no idea how to handle these next few days.

The answer is that there is no "how to." You handle *it*, and it handles *you*, and other people help every step of the way. You surprise yourself with how strong you can be, how strong your parents are, and how you're all sort of exactly the same person. You find that you pull pieces of wisdom and words of support from the strangest places (for me most of the screenplay of *Steel Magnolias* – a movie I watched roughly twice a week from 3rd to 6th grades. Yes, bizarre for a 3rd grader, but now I just keep channeling Sally Field in the rough moments, which is working fairly well). And you learn – though you only realize it when you sit down to write – that pieces of this moment are exactly the kind of thing you almost need, in a so-strange way, to get you *through* the rest of your 20's.

You know that close family is a gift but you don't really see it in action until a moment as binding as death. Once you've experienced what that support system can provide, you know you'll shift anything and everything around to keep it a priority from here on out. You've heard what 60+ years of marriage can mean to a couple and their family, but when you see that in this last stage of life any thoughts of never marrying or just settling on someone are gone. You've heard that it's nice if a big family stays in the same general area, but until every single immediate family member is in the hospital room and not a flight away, you don't realize you can probably deal with New Jersey.

Now that I'm going through the motions of this loss, I know that my reaction is to shift into keep-myself-busy mode to avoid sitting in the sadness. I know that I actually don't want to have a tantrum or run away -- I just want to keep my sisters around me at all times to make sure they're okay. And I know that I'd probably prefer to make it all the way through my 20's without having this happen, but all I keep thinking about are those silver linings that make it 1/2 devastating but the other half an important life lesson.

All in all that makes me a fairly even combo of my Mom, my Mommom, and *Steel Magnolia's* Sally Field, which may be the greatest lesson of all.

Ed Note: I continue to miss my Mommom during so many moments of so many days, but am pleased to say that her husband, my Poppop, is still going strong at 91-years-old. Despite the preparation that first experience with loss provided and my subsequent years of general growth, I am in no way prepared to lose him.

How And Why Rachel Is Never Single

from 7/22/09

I haven't seen my friend Rachel in four or five months, but there's no question in my mind that she's dating someone. She's always dating someone. In the 12 - *wow has it been that long*?? - years I've known her, she's only *not* been dating someone for a few months at a time, and even then she has a prospect. It's important to note that these aren't one-off relationships. These are deep, meaningful relationships with people that she remains friends with 80-90% of the time.

We were talking about this situation -- her dating situation -- over salads in Madison Square Park the other day. I was saying that above paragraph except put "you" in place of "she" and change whatever other pronouns you need to, and she was saying things like this:

- **Rachel**: It's because I ask these people out.
- **Me:** Hhmm. Elaborate.
- **Rachel**: I determine I like someone and then I say, "I like you, do you want to go on a date?"
- **Me**: I'm sorry, what?
- **Rachel**: Yeah, or sometimes I say, "I think you're cute. Let's go on a date."
- **Me**: And then what?
- **Rachel**: They either say OK or something like, "now's not a good time for me," or whatever they want to say if they don't want to go out with me.
- **Me:** Right, Makes sense. So w*hen* do you do this?
- **Rachel**: As soon as I can usually. I mean, why would I waste my time if they don't like me or I end up going on a date and not liking them? And what if I don't ask them and then someone else does first?

It's hard to respond to all that because all of those things are *absolutely* true and yet never factor into my thought process as I'm too busy thinking, "well, now could be a good time but my hair is in a bun and generally looks better in a low, side pony so I should probably wait to make my move."

Do I want to waste my time? No, never. But would I rather waste three full years rather than be embarrassed for three full minutes? Yes, absolutely except more like six...years. Aren't I ever worried that someone else is going to get them first? Stop *saying* that! You might make it happen!

Rachel didn't stop at that, of course. She wanted to be sure to present so much logic and statistical success that I might be shamed into listening to her. *Might*, of course, because we all know strong logic and clear statistical evidence is no match for but-what-if-I-have-to-see-him-in-a-bar-within-a-year-from-the-rejection?!?!

- **Rachel**: I mean, bottom line, I am a strong person and I want to be a strong person in a relationship. So I want people to know that up front, which is why I pursue them, so it's clear that I'm bold and fairly confident. And I only want to date people who are comfortable with confident people so it always works out. Almost all of my relationships have been with someone who really liked that I was confident. And I think almost every single one of those relationships started because I approached the person.

I need to pause to call out the fact that Rachel is a lesbian. I mention this now and not at the top of the post because if I had you'd have read the entire post thinking, "yeah but she's a lesbian so it's totally different." Pieces of "it" (here representing the dynamic between the same sex in dating vs. opposite sexes) may be different, yes. But the most significant among them is that Rachel isn't accountable to specific gender roles that wedge us into place. *Straight girls shouldn't ask guys out*, some thought processes still hold. *Straight guys don't want to be with obviously more dominant woman* is a frequent school of thought. So yes, Rachel isn't approaching this from exactly the same set up as guy/girl daters, but that doesn't change the *logic* it only changes the stereotype and expectation.

Everything about her "why I do it" makes sense. People who like confident people like that they're confident. People show that they're confident and bold by making first moves. Successful relationships are the result of people being true to themselves. And further, if you ask people out that *you* like you can determine if they like you. Yes, evaluating their Facebook behavior, watching them like a hawk while in bars, consulting every single one of your friends on the issue, and booby trapping them with fake dates may also help you figure out if they like you, but read all that again and tell me how you feel about yourself?

Two minutes of maybe awkward and it can *allll* be over. It's very, *very* convincing, isn't it? Every "but what if..." running through your mind is right: you could get rejected, you could be embarrassed, you could feel super awkward around that person in the future, but then it's done, and nine times out of ten you'll grow apart and move on because the only reason you were associating with the person was to continue to evaluate if they like you too.

- **Rachel**: I mean, listen, it doesn't work for everyone. Some people just can't handle it.

Oh no she didn't... Can we not *handle* asking someone out? No. What we can't handle is ourselves if they say no. It's a small but significant difference.

And thank you Rachel. You're a frustration to us all.

Ed Note: In April of 2013 I attended the wedding of this good friend Rachel to her now wife, Mel. Rachel met Mel at her synagogue, admired her from afar for as little time as possible, and then promptly asked her out before anyone else could get in the way.

My Mom, Me and Choice

from 8/7/09

Today I turn the age my Mom was when she had me – 26-years-old.

I wonder if it's a uniquely female thing for that to matter – to arrive at the age your Mom was when she became a mother and go "*whoa.*"

I like to think of myself as a mature adult, a fairly together person. I'm proud of myself a coupe times a week. When difficult things come my way, I find that I can deal with them sans tantrums. In general, I am doing what people would call "well." Do I act 26? Most of the time. Do I feel 26? Sure, I guess I'd say I do. But could I have a child at some point during this 26th year of my life?

OHMYGODNO. NO NO NO NO *NO.*

Do I know how to care for a baby? Yes, enough. I have those three little sisters you've heard so much about. Would I *destroy* the life of a child? No, not at all. I know all my lullabies by heart. It's just that 95% of my life would have to change drastically in order to shift from my current mode – let's call it work/write/drink/eat/fun mode – to bear-and-care for children mode. I believe that involves saving money/not sleeping/Mom jeans/and an elevator building if not actual back yard, right?

I cannot do that right now because I don't want to that right now.

Not having children is a choice at any age, but so is every piece of the single, 26-year-old lifestyle. At 26 I remain un-beholden to anyone but myself (and my family because I love them, but even that's a choice). I make decisions every day that affect the kind of 26-year-old I am.

I live in New York City making my savings account similar to a not-so-funny joke. I work in the media industry meaning long hours and low pay. I write as much as I can on the side, which makes for early mornings and some very late nights. I have a close network of friends so all remaining spare time is spent organizing things to do with that group.

I could write less. I could make more money at a different job. I could spend differently (namely less...). I could be in a relationship (I maintain that most people *could* be in a relationship if *any* relationship was the goal). But I would have to adjust lots of little pieces of my life to shift into making those things possible.

No, not everything is planned, but most major decisions come at the cost of something else. I believe these are referred to as *sacrifices*, but that's always sounded like such a bummer. Let's call them cause/effects.

The question is when do those cause/effects start to shift? When do you know it's time to put one priority above another, especially as you're turning the corner on your mid-twenties and people are starting to say, "you know, you're not getting any younger.." (Was I ever??).

You hear people say, "then I decided to settle down," or, "it was around then that I knew it was time to be in a relationship," or, "I just knew the time was right for a career change." How do they know? What happens?

As I was thinking about turning 26 – and what my Mom was doing as she was turning 26 (her birthday is in June, so she was doing 7-months-pregnant things), I thought about what I'd be willing to give up to get some of the things some other 26-year-olds have.

What causes would I take up to affect other results? Would I trade X to have Y or Z? Would I shift my attention from A to B so I could make my way to C? If someone told me I could have _____, but I'd have to stop my _____, would I do it?

We are the sum of our choices – trite but true - from as early on as we understand the concept of choice. But I think we sometimes forget that in choosing one thing, we're also choosing *not* another. This isn't an argument against having "it all" (There's no argument. You can't, but that's for another day). This is just a newly 26-year-old woman (who still feels like she should be referred to as "girl") realizing what she loves about her life but what she could and might soon leave behind now that the future changes focus with each passing year.

Ed Note: As I write this I am a little over a month from turning 30. At 30, my mom had two children and another on the way. I currently have zero children and even less on the way. Much has changed since my 26th birthday. I'm now an engaged woman living three thousand miles from home and finally pursuing the career I've aspired to for years, but I don't know if I'm any closer to being ready to have a child. I am financially closer. I am physically closer (as in, I need to have one sooner than I did before…), but I don't know if I'm emotionally closer.

Do you ever know? Is there ever the exact right time?

I guess I'll have to report back in the 30-Nothing version of this book – unless I'm too busy raising a litter of kids to write one…

How To Go From Friends To More Than Friends

from 9/21/09

The process of transitioning from being friends to being more than friends is the third most difficult challenge known to modern man. (1. How to establish universal health care in the U.S. 2. How to bring peace about in the Middle East, and 3. How to tell your best guy friend that you actually wish he was your boyfriend. 4. Opening plastic packaging for certain electronic devices).

Every seven seconds some girl somewhere starts crying because she doesn't know how to tell "that guy" she has feelings for him (note: I made that stat up, but it feels correct). It's a total mess out there. Should she even do it? What if she does it and he doesn't have feelings for her? Obviously the friendship is ruined! What if she doesn't do it, and he does have feelings for her, and they just never end up together because both of them are too chicken to say something? Isn't there just a way to figure this out indirectly so there's no slash low risk and everyone ends up happy?

Allow me to Bounty extra quilted this situation:

Yes. It doesn't matter. Right, exactly. And No.

Of course there's more, but here is my blanket statement on the issue that appears as opinion but is fact, fact:

If you have very strong romantic feelings for one of your close male friends you should either make those feelings clear *or* stop being such good friends. I support the former in most cases, but do as you please.

Why? Because of another blanket statement that seems like an opinion but is actually 100% truth:

If you have very strong romantic feelings for one of your close male friends and *don't* make them clear or stop being such good friends, the friendship - as it is at least - will eventually end anyway. Here's why:

A friendship in which one party is in love with the other is not a friendship - it's a unique social situation where one person is engaged in friendship while the other is engaged in a life mission to figure out if their love is returned. As such that person (a girl for example's sake) often behaves less like a true friend and more like an actress - an actress cast in the role of this guy's girlfriend. Does said female actually want this person as a friend in her life? Yes. Would she continue to want him if she was 100% certain he did not currently and would never love her back? No.

That's what makes this "friendship" ripe for destruction. Half of its members don't want it to continue existing like it is and have ultimate designs to change it. As such they frequently find themselves doing things that are designed to appear *friendly* in nature but are actually plots to figure out what's really going on inside the other guy's head. Such as: Let me bring him around my guy friends from college so he can see that I treat him differently than I treat him and realize maybe I *like*-like him. Or: Let me invite that guy I met at the bar last week to his birthday party so I can see if he acts jealous. Or the oh-so-common: let me invite him to go Flea Market shopping so he can see me in my adorable Flea Market shopping outfit and realize that he really does love me, and then his overwhelming love will prompt him to just tell me!

Yes, it's as exhausting as it sounds. And no, it can't go on like that forever. That's where the destruction part comes in, and it comes in one of three forms.

1. You crack.

Alcohol plus years of denied feelings can/will/often lead to slurred confessions, blackout "moves", and you telling his roommate everything and begging for advice. I've never seen all three go down, but I wouldn't put it past someone.

2. He starts dating someone who isn't you. (Hopefully this happens before you crack...)

3. He does love you back, somehow this just becomes very clear, you start dating, and it's as it always should have been.

Now here's why, no matter which of those happen, it's for the best.

1a. No it is not easy to recover from drunk confessing that you love someone. Yes things will take some time to be back to normal, if they ever go back to normal. But this is good because they 100% needed to change. You cannot and should not remain as close as you were to this person! It's crazy, self destructive and preventing you from being with someone with whom you'll have a reciprocated relationship. So method: negative. Effects: awkward. End result: correct. Sorry.

2a. Yes you will feel pain if he starts dating someone new, but like the above, it will get you where you need to be – out of a co-dependent relationship with a friend you want to date. To reiterate: friends you want to date aren't friends, they're projects.

3a. I've heard this "it just worked out" situations happens. I believe it's possible. I haven't experienced it directly or indirectly, but if you find yourself in this lucky situation, I'd start looking out for falling pianos.

Moral of the story: you need to change this relationship. You can change it with a heart-felt letter that holds the option of response ("If you feel the same way, let me know. If you don't, let's spend six to eight months not speaking. Thanks!"). You can change it with a drunken confession to his best friend that gets back to him, and then awkwardly back to you. Or you can let it die and slowly back your way out of the friendship (sometimes if the writing is on the wall, this is the best decision). But the situation will eventually run its course, and whatever happens between you two further down the road might have a lot to do with how you handle the crossroads.

And yes, I know the title of this post is "how" to go from friends to more. That was a device to draw you in. If I titled it, "why going from friends to more is really, really difficult and offers few examples of success, *but* you should still get it over with and tell him already!" you'd probably X this post out and return to examining what girls have recently written on his Facebook wall...

Ed Note: I will now – thanks to distance and a fiancé – share that I have confessed my feelings to two of the three friends who I secretly wished were more. The first turned out to be gay (but I like to believe he loves me just as much back, still), the second turned out to have just started dating the woman he eventually married (making my confession in the rain outside a New York City subway stop one of our last interactions), and the third has stayed a good friend because I realized it was ultimately not meant to be and changed the nature of our friendship before it all blew up in my face. So, yes, there's a man among you who never knew and never will – unless he always did.

Phone Calls: Chivalry or Pleated Pants?

from 11/11/09

Date: Last Wednesday
Time: 2:30PM
Location: GChat
Note: This conversation has been pasted in its entirety without corrections to anything, though that will quickly become obvious.

Chris:
question for you
well
statement
and id like your reaction
me: ok
Chris: "i think the young culture has gotten to a point where calling has become chivalrous"
me: agree
firmly
Chris: kind of awful
me: really, really awful
but really true
Chris: has calling become a turn-off?
me: no
I think it's become an easy way to really show someone you care
Chris: but it's not a turnoff?
me: not for me
Chris: in the age of flings and detachment, isnt it too formal?
me: but girls aren't all the same
And I'd prefer the age of flings and detachment end
frankly
Chris: ha, praise the gospel sister
me: so if I called a guy

and that annoyed him a ton
I'd stop seeing him
and if you call a girl
and she's like, "ew why is he *calling* me"
she's a bitch
Chris: yeah
i think people equate calling with pleated pants
me: HAHA
that's so fucking sad
Chris: they both exist, and some people use them both, but mostly just older people out of touch with style
me: well I'm fighting that
I feel like this calls for one of those SNL Weekend Update segments where they go *really?! REALLY?!* Calling someone on the phone is a *turn-off?! REALLY?!!?!*

(As you can see, it was a super busy day at the office for me)

Sometimes in order to understand the random, crap details of dating, you have to reverse into things. So instead of, "should I make X move," or, "should I make Y gesture," it's *if* I make X move or Y gesture and the person is turned off, what does that say about the person I'm pursuing?

Applied to this issue that would read as, "if I decide to call the girl I'm interested in dating versus just text her *and* she's totally turned off by that, what does that mean?"

It means one of two things. 1. She is a sad, strange woman who's lost all ability to talk on the phone. 2. She's not into you. Call me harsh, but there's not a WORLD in which someone should say, "I was really liking him but then he *called* me, like on the *phone*. I mean, can we say dealbreaker??"

Same applies the other way around. If you're calling a guy incessantly, and he's calling you back a tad less, fine. He's a guy. They don't love the phone. But if you're calling a guy every so often and he's exclusively texting you back, that's weird slash rude. Also, if a guy ever says to you, "I think talking on the phone is out-dated," run for the hills.

It's the phone, people. Think of it like having a conversation in person except with technology that allows you to be in two *different places.* Is talking on the phone antiquated? Yes. Does that mean doing it has turned into a turn-off? I'm going to say no. Really no. Please, please, please really no…

Ed Note: I'm afraid to say that the frequency of phone calls has only lessened since I wrote this post. In fact, my little sister once told me that she's never been asked out by a man via his voice. In other words, she has only ever been asked out via text, Gchat or Facebook message. So, maybe it's over? Maybe we'll all stop talking on the phone in all circumstances, not just dating?

To me, that would be incredibly sad. When R and I first met he called me on the phone a few times a week just to chat. We were currently living across the country from each other, but I'd venture to say I got to know him better through those dozens of phone calls than I would have if we met for a few dates at a dark bar, and it was certainly better than if he'd texted me everything he was saying. Call me pleated pants, but I stand by that belief.

An Open Letter To Anyone Who Knows Anyone About To End A Relationship

from 10/4/09

Dear everyone who falls within the above category and/or the actual people contemplating ending whatever you have going on with someone:

First - really sorry to hear that, and I hope you slash this friend of yours learned something valuable from the relationship and well done for getting into one in the first place *yadda, yadda*.

Second and more importantly - if you are a person someone seeks counsel from before ending their relationship, as in you find yourself on the other side of the table from someone going, "so...yeah...I think I need to take a step back from it...probably end it. It just isn't there. Not sure why, but it's not happening for me..." I on behalf of all mankind am *begging* you to make them do so in a respectful manner (we'll get to what that means).

Samely (whatever, it should be a word) - if you are the breaker-upper, I am doing the same degree of begging for you to man up and end it in a way that is as least hurtful as possible.

To take a step back - I get it. It sucks to end it with someone. It's awkward. You know you're hurting their feelings a little slash a lot. You know it's going to be a really uncomfortable conversation. You don't *want* to lie, but the truth sounds so mean and dumb. You're like, shit what if they *cry!?* Oh my god I cannot handle it if they cry! It's just this annoying, miserable thing that there's never the right moment for and so you put it off a week or a month or a year until the person you're breaking up with goes, "so, hey, is something wrong? You seem...different..." And even then you're so consumed with all the shit they're going to say about you after you end it that you let it go a few weeks more. I get it. I've been there. I've done it wrong, too.

But here's the thing(s):

- Their feelings will be infinitely more hurt if you pull the, "one-week-disappearing-act-blow-off," (working title).

- It's going to be a *waaaay* more uncomfortable conversation if it starts with them saying, "hey, so I got your text saying you think we should stop seeing each other, but I wanted to talk that through over the phone seeing as though we're adults..."

- Whether you tell the truth or tell a little lie, it's not going to sound nearly as dumb as, "sorry I know I should have addressed this instead of just ignoring you for two weeks but, well, I didn't know how to deal with it."

- And trust me, they're going to talk considerably more shit about you if you do it like a dick versus a sincere person.

I know it's hard to see the forest through trees on this one, especially if you're ending something that wasn't really official, or ending something with a generally great person, or ending something because - bottom line - you met someone better. There is no *great* way to go about it but - and here is the crux of my point - there are really, *really* shitty ways. Don't do those.

So, to the friends on the other end of the table I'm saying push hard and use threats if necessary. Because remember, you are closely associated with this person, so this stands the chance of making you look really bad too.

And to you, if you so happen to be in this situation: again, I'm sorry. But I'm not sorry enough to excuse you from treating someone you dated like someone you barely know and definitely don't respect. So if you're really that incapable of dealing with this like an adult, please see the below email template. Good luck!

Subject line: (Ed Note: this part's on you...)

Hey _____,

Listen, I've been giving some thought to what we've had going on for the past few (*choose duration of time. Ed note: if it's years you close that email and go do this in person, asshole*), and I realize that I (*choose one*): need some time to myself/don't have my heart in it/am in a place where I don't want to be in a relationship/feel like we have a lot of differences, so I think we should stop seeing each other.

I'm incredibly sorry to say this over email, but I can't handle telling you in person or over the phone because I am a weak person. Sorry, and I wish you all the best.

Take care!

Ed Note: Between the time I wrote this post and the time I met the man I will now marry I was not in a relationship that warranted a break-up, so I can't personally say whether or not the situation has improved out there. I'd venture to guess that it hasn't, so I believe the above advice stands. Also, call me old-fashioned, but I'd like to clarify that the above e-mail should be sent via actual e-mail, not Facebook messager, Gchat or a very long text.

Kennedy And The Superior Set Up

from 10/14/09

"Hey! Jessie! I'm so pumped! I thought of a bunch of stories to tell you so I can finally make the blog!" Kennedy said to me 1.5 minutes after I arrived at dinner. He was eight to ten people down from me at a ten to twelve person table positioned in a room so loud he had to yell it for me to hear. This did not stop him.

I haven't seen Kennedy in approx two years *aaanndd* had no idea he reads this blog, but post material and straight, male fans are two things I'd be foolish to refuse. Unfortunately Kennedy was too drunk to get out more than one story. Fortunately, for his fifteen minutes of fame at least, it was a good one.

Kennedy works in an office where he has important superiors. These are superiors you not only want to please but also want to curry favor with (if that is in fact the saying...) whenever possible. One such superior had taken interest in Kennedy's dating life and, upon finding out that Kennedy didn't currently have a dating life, *strongly* recommended he go on a date with a fellow employee. This is where I'm fuzzy, but somehow this person works *among* Kennedy but not directly with him such that the superior thought it totally appropriate for them to date. Bottom line, the boss gave the green light.

"So here's the thing." he tells me, now from the seat directly next to mine where I unexpectedly found him after I returned from the bathroom, "She's *fine* looking. *Fine*. Not *bad*. Just *fine*...you know what I'm saying?"

"Yes," I said, "I know what you're saying."

"Like *fiiine*, but not *great*. Like, maybe *great* to some guys, but just *fiine* to me," he said.

"Yep," I said, "got it."

And then he said something to even *further* clarify his very clear point that I won't repeat here sos not to tarnish his moment in the spotlight.

The issue: this superior wants very badly to make the set up happen, but Kennedy knows he's not really interested in dating this girl. He'd be fine if something maybe happened with this girl after, say, the company Christmas party, but a formal date - especially one initiated by this important superior - would be a bad idea - "right?" he asked.

"Very right," I said.

Next he wanted to discuss his options. At this point dinner was over and we were all just figuring out how to split the check twelve ways. I zone out the moment this charade starts. This time I considered Kennedy's options as I averted dinner bill math.

- Tell the absolute truth to this very important boss? "Thanks so much, sir, but this girl you think is perfect for me is actually not my type at all."

- Lie to get out of it? "Thank you so much, sir, but I actually *just* started seeing someone, so it wouldn't be appropriate for me to go out with this girl."

- Or just take the recommendation, go, and make something up afterwards? "Thank you so much again, sir. We had a nice time, but I've just recently decided to become a vegetarian, and she's not, and I think it would be too difficult for me to date her at this time."

Let's take a pause while I disclaim the answer I'm about to give.

I understand that lying is not appropriate in most-to-all circumstances. It is wrong, inherently, and I know this. That said I believe that there are circumstances where you are best served by telling a variation on the absolute truth that mitigates strong, negative issues all parties involved would experience by telling the absolute truth. Case in point, this case (or do I just say "case in point."?... I never know…)

No good is going to come from Kennedy telling this superior that he's just not attracted to the girl. He could very well say, "you know sir - thanks so much - but she's just not my type. I actually prefer _____ girls," but that's just going to open the floodgates for this superior to set Kennedy up with every _____ girl he knows. At the same time, a lie as blatant as, "sorry, I'm actually seeing someone," is just going to bite Kennedy in the ass because the superior clearly has no problem meddling in work people's love lives. And so - in my opinion - Kennedy is left with one slightly weird option that, technically speaking, is a lie. It's this: "Thanks sir - appreciate you thinking of me - but I have a strict no-dating-anyone-associated-with-work policy. Just a personal rule, so I'm going to have to say no to the idea of the set-up."

Yes, this superior may protest. He may say, "Come on! I authorize it! Everyone around here does it," and that may be true, but Kennedy has every right to head the warning of the don't-shit-where-you-eat principal. The superior will have to respect that. Game over.

And yes, Kennedy may some day find himself in a compromising position with someone from the office, but in that case he can either keep it quiet or plead blackout drunk.

I gave Kennedy this advice as we were leaving the restaurant, but I'm not sure he got every detail straight. Luckily this story became his blog premiere, so it's all captured right here for him to review at any time.

Thanks Kennedy. Great to see you. And let me know when you

want to talk through the rest of the bunch of stories.

Ed Note: I had absolutely no idea what Kennedy did about the above situation, until I e-mailed him to find out and insist he write the addendum to this post. Here, several years later and far more sober, is Kennedy's addendum:

I was lucky enough to corner Jessie, spill my story, and get solid advice, all before my night abruptly ended at about 10PM due to a bit too many pre-dinner festivities. As for the actual story, I sort of took a middle path to the three options laid out by Jessie. Rather than outright rejecting this offer of matchmaking, lying about seeing someone, or agreeing to be set up, I just never followed up with the offer and it sort of fell by the wayside - out of sight out of mind sort of thing. In retrospect, I feel that my characterization came across to Jessie much too harsh (probably all those pre-dinner festivities…). In truth, the woman in question a lovely young lady who, according to Facebook, recently got married. As for myself, I got engaged this past winter to the love of my life. So in the end, Jessie's advice turned out for the best for everyone involved. As for my superior, while I no longer work with him, he remains a friend and one of my most important mentors. So Jessie, this story has a happy ending and I am glad you were there to point me in the right direction!

Second Ed Note: I was personally hoping for something way more salacious where Kennedy made the absolute wrong move and ended up offending the girl, pissing off the boss and getting reprimanded if not fired, but now that my days of exploiting friends' love lives for a blog are over, I guess it's cool that Kennedy ended up really happy and gainfully employed.

The Bullshit of Opportunity Cost

from 3/31/10

I spent a few hours yesterday afternoon Gchatting with a friend who wants to leave his job to pursue a life of not his job. We discussed how exactly he'd go about making money should he leave. For the time being said friend needs to keep his current job, so he'll stay identified as "a friend."

This friend is one of those modern renaissance men - a writer, graphic artist, video-producing stage manager type who's dabbled in theater and fashion (if you count be-dazzling suspenders for a Lady Gaga concert, which you should). He has a good job writing for a major publication. It's a job many people would die for and one that could become a fantastic career. Problem is, it's not a job *he* would die for or a career he wants. And to make matters more frustrating, it's one of those "incredible opportunity" jobs, which in Manhattan is code for pays-shit-and-consumes-your-life.

What does he want? He isn't sure, but it definitely doesn't fall inside the box of traditional careers. "Well, will staying at this job help you in this or other careers?" I asked him, as we played *20 Questions: Should-I-leave-my-job? Edition*.

"No," he responded, "Because I don't want a career."

It was the most honest and relatable thing I'd heard in a very long time.

A career - the way most people think of it - is a trajectory inside a sector of employment. You have a career in journalism, a career in media, a successful career in law, education, or finance. You pick a path and march up its ladder toward whatever levels you can reach. Specific things get you there, specific things don't – the end.

This friend isn't interest in any one thing with any one title. He wants to create some things, participate in creating some others, then figure out what he likes next and go make some of that. Maybe that means writing? Designing? Producing? Entrepreneuring? He doesn't know, and right now that's not his question. His question is how he's supposed to get to any of that if his 9-to-9's are spent slaving at a career he doesn't want for a paycheck that amounts to little more than what he'd make at a Baby Gap (Actual figures. We did the math).

"Your opportunity cost is out of whack," I told him as we discussed the merits of staying versus going. "Even though you have a good situation at a good company, what they're paying you isn't worth what they're costing you in opportunity. That's their fault."

"Yeah, but it's my problem," he said, and he was unfortunately right.

If that isn't the plight of the 20-something "creative" I don't know what is.

We (well, many among us) need jobs for money and money for survival. So we get jobs that make sense and offer potentially great career projection. Then we decide we don't want the careers we're projecting towards, but don't know how to A. figure out how to make money off what we do want or B. figure out how to make better money to make the current job more worthwhile.

Find me a job that pays tons and takes very little time and effort (but isn't being a professional egg donor), and I'll get you a list of would-be creatives begging for a chance to interview. Unfortunately those jobs don't really exist.

So then the question - and my friend's question - becomes one of those simple ones that's annoyingly impossible to answer: How much is your current grind preventing you from getting what you really want? Enough to make what little money you're paid totally worthless? Enough to make you leave it behind to tend bar or serve coffee? How much do you *not* want your current career to leave it behind and pursue life from 24 on without one?

All we truly need to survive is some money, some health insurance, a place to live, and Top Ramen to eat. So then for my friend the question becomes not if he should step out of the rat race but *how?* You can't Google, how to leave job and become creator of TBD things (but if you do - just for fun – the first result you'll get is Steve Job's Wikipedia page, *which is genius*).

Opportunity cost is a tricky bitch in the life of this city's 24-year-olds. The "careers" of the world have you by the balls, the Baby Gaps employ a steady stream of actors, and "creator" isn't something you can list on a LinkedIn profile.

So what's a guy like my friend to do? I don't know, but we'll figure it out. And in the meantime, if I read the TIME "What the Healthcare Bill means for you" article correctly - at least he's still young enough to get covered under his parent's health insurance.

Ed Note: It took me almost four years after writing this post to leave my own unwanted career to pursue my passions. In those four years I contemplated leaving to do everything from walk dogs or babysit children to serve grande soy lattes (because FYI, Starbucks offers health insurance to employees who work 40+ hours per week).

There are a lot of reasons that I didn't leave, many of which are rooted in fear and financials, but once I finally did quit I couldn't believe I hadn't taken the plunge sooner. You don't know what you're capable of accomplishing until complete failure is staring you straight in the face. It's not unlike anything in life – the degree to which you want it is in direct correlation to what you're willing to do to go get it. If those percentages are skewed, you won't make a move. But once they're properly aligned, you can't move fast enough.

Oh, and re: my friend. He spent two years living in New Orleans and almost a year living in Los Angeles before deciding to return to New York. His path continues to be windy and by no means business card title driven, but he's no longer stuck, and that can be the most important step of all.

What I'm Worth To The Men of Murray Hill

from 4/16/10

I survived my first dating auction. Would I say it was miserable? No, not at all. Would I say I want to do another one today slash ever? No, absolutely not, ever.

Here's how it all went down.

Van Diemen's bar - the scene of the big show - is located in Manhattan's infamous Murray Hill 'hood. For those familiar with that neighborhood and its population of men, I *know*... For those unfamiliar, think of it as a 10-block college campus except instead of classrooms and dorms it's just bars, plus everyone technically graduated three to ten years ago.

I arrived to a teaming crowd of co-eds holding identical pieces of paper and staring at everyone who walked in with an uncanny, "is that person for sale?" look. Immediate thoughts: Who else is getting auctioned off? Are their outfits cuter than mine? Where am I going to have to stand? Is where I'm going to have to stand going to work with my outfit?

My friend Julie was at the door with wrist-bands for drink specials (the answer is, it takes three vodka sodas to prepare to be sold in public) and a stack of those identical pieces of paper - an "auction items" summary featuring mini pictures and mini bios describing us bait to the masses.

It is weird to have a hundred or so people holding your picture and trying to match it with your face. It is weirder when you overhear them saying, "that girl seem pretty good." But it is weird-*est* when one of them comes up to you and says, "Jessie? Good. I'm going to win you."

Now, having given obsessive thought to the intricacies of the dating auction, I decided that sale order was of primary importance. You do not want to go first. You do not want to go last. But even more importantly, you do not want to go after someone incredibly good-looking or with an obvious fan base in the audience. I quickly assessed the crowd, crosschecked it against the "tips sheet," and then begged the organizers to switch me from fifth to third position. Some girl named "Liz" looked way too promising to follow.

8:15pm - two vodka sodas in - Girl One takes the stage. She's blonde, longhaired and adorable in an Anne-of-Green-Gables-takes-Manhattan sort of way. She's wearing a very short, black, long-sleeved dress belted at the waist. In other words, she's the opposite of the girl you want to go after. I silently curse myself for thinking "Liz" was a bigger issue than this chick. You never can trust a 2x2" black-and-white Facebook photo…

After an excruciating five to eight minutes of the MC begging ("Let's go guys! This is for Cancer!!!…research…CANCER RESEARCH!), Girl One coyly smiling (it's really hard to perfect a please-buy-me!!....but-not-you-over-there look), and me drinking an entire third vodka soda (no comment), the biding was closed. Girl One went for an incredibly respectable $80.

At this point I contemplated falling down and getting hurt. Girl One was up there for a LONG time. Just *standing* there, smiling-*ish* but mostly looking like get-me-off-this-f-ing-stage. And $80 is a LOT of dollars. I mean, I planted friends in the audience, but not ones willing to waste 80 bones on a fake bid.

"How are you feeling?!" my friend Lillian asked as Girl One came down off the stage.

"Not good," I said through my mini drink straw.

I'm told that Guy Two went for about $125, but I was too busy practicing standing, holding a drink, and looking amazing to pay much attention. $125 is most certainly more than I ever imaged I'd go for, but again, Guy Two was up there for a *long* time. Longer than I'd ever prefer to be standing in one place while a group of my peers decide whether or not they want to pay money to own me for an evening.

And then, it was my turn. GULP.

The "stage" was actually a flight of stairs facing the crowd, so naturally I almost fell up them upon taking my position. Then the MC introduced me as being from Boston - *not* a New York crowd-pleaser (also, not true), and finally, he started the bidding at $50 - higher than Girl One at $30 and Boy One at $40. Earlier in the night I told my friend Brian (one of the saints who came to bid in case things got really ugly) that I just wanted to go for $30, and here I was starting at the cost of a UNIQLO cashmere sweater!!! Disaster...or so I thought.

See, there are friends who will hold your hair back when you get sick, and those are really good friends. Then there are friends who will go with you to an outer borough for an obligatory birthday party, and those are great friends. But the friends who will scream "she's worth it, trust me!!!" when you take the stage, start a four-man biding war, drive your sale price up to $220 in three minutes, and swoop in with a $240 selling price so the creepy-guy-you-don't-know in the corner doesn't win you - those are the best friends of all.

I sold for $240 to a good friend slash co-worker (and thank *god* for that), but there were some hands raised in the audience as the price climbed that were most certainly not (yet) acquaintances. It's hard to mask a look of who-are-you-out-there-that-just-bid-$175-to-date-me??? I just focused on smiling, nodding and not falling down the stairs.

How do you know whether or not you succeeded in your first-ever dating auction? Hard to say, but if the girl who's supposed to go after you says, "I hate you...I mean, good job," you can figure you did okay.

And re: those mystery guys with the high bids. I kindly thanked them all for their interest in purchasing me. None seemed like quite the right fit for a follow-up date, but I did appreciate their monetary affirmation of my person (Word to the wise: being the almost-winner in a dating auction is a genius way to meet girls.)

In the end, it was a success for a great cause with far less pain that I imaged through my vivid nightmares for three weeks prior to the event. I just could *definitely* have done without the, "I thought you looked like the girl from *Glee*, and I totally want to bang her," confession from "Dave" who was apparently willing to pay $175 to try with me.

Ed Note: That was, in fact, my first and last dating auction, though it's worth noting that several years later I had a dream that I was a contestant at a similar event. In the dream Andrew Keegan won me in a bidding war against my first grade crush, Jared Higley. Makes sense.

Moving Out To Move Up

from 4/19/10

I'm moving out of Manhattan this week.

On Thursday night my dad will (attempt to) park the minivan outside my building and help me cart four years down the four flights from my Greenwich Village apartment. Then I'll make him knock me unconscious before we drive away from my beloved neighborhood en route to the place I'll be calling home for the summer – *home* - specifically, suburban New Jersey - more specifically, a second floor bedroom I'll share with my 20-year-old sister.

All together now: deep breath in…deep breath out…

On Thursday I'm moving out of my Manhattan apartment and into a bedroom in my parent's New Jersey home that I'll share with my little sister.

As my friend Paul said, "Ouch girl! This story better be good."

Thing is, there isn't really a *story*. Four plus years ago I moved into a $900 a month 28th Street sublet on a 30K salary; I had zero savings. Six months later I moved into a new sublet, $50 more expensive, on that same income, still zero savings. In a year I switched jobs to a 35K gig and my rent increased to $1,000. Now three jobs into life, my salary has increased but not significantly enough for me to save any real sum of money. The debt I incurred in those years of very little income is something I chip away at monthly. Add in college loans and typical life costs, and I'm certainly getting *by* but not comfortably. I still live paycheck to paycheck.

I mention these really personal details because they're shared by so many 20-something city-dwellers pursuing careers in industries with low pay scales. These are desirable and important jobs, jobs we work hard to get and hard at once we've gotten, so there's no regret involved. It's just the way that world works, and if you want in you have to be willing to take the good with the bad. I am not financially secure, and I know many of you aren't either.

It dawned on me a few months ago as I contemplated what the next five years of my life might hold, that every possibility I can image or change I might desire is limited by my financial situation. I don't have a safety net. I don't have a cushion. And so there are ideas, projects or changes that I can't even entertain because I don't have the means. I have to keep peddling, and really, I should seek opportunities that make financial sense. Read: I should sell out.

That's not okay with me. I don't want to feel trapped. I don't want to feel beholden. I don't want to miss out on exploration and travel because I can't afford it. And more importantly, I don't want to throw it on a credit card, and I can't just ask my parents for an 8K nest egg.

When I first graduated from college my primary goal was to keep life as much like college as possible. I didn't know what lay ahead, but I knew I needed to be as social and active as possible - to dive in and live life in the city. My concerns were not financial, and I wasn't frustrated by having to pinch pennies.

Now my priorities have changed. I'm secure in my friendship and comfortable in my job. I can navigate the city and myself. I know when it's time to go home versus when it's time to switch to shots. I could continue to pinch pennies. I could get by for years without solid savings, but I don't want to anymore, and thanks to a family that has room, patience and a house commuting distance from the city, I don't have to.

A lot of post-grads spend their first years after college living at home to get on their feet and lay the groundwork for an eventual move. I'm taking a bit of a different approach - a sort of mid-20's city sabbatical. From now until I'm-not-sure-when, a subletter will fill my spot as I experiment with a departure from my fast-track life and to a more savings-oriented lifestyle. I don't know what will happen at the end of the summer. Maybe I'll move right back into my apartment, or maybe I'll move somewhere else, but whatever I do will be what I want most because I'll have the options to follow that desire.

This is difficult on a number of levels. It's difficult because I have a co-dependent relationship with Manhattan and, more specifically, Thompson Street between Bleecker and West 3rd. But outside of the obvious I'm-going-to-hate-commuting sentiments, it's difficult because part of me feels like a failure. I haven't been entirely responsible. I haven't taken the most sensible jobs. I have followed my passions versus my logic, and those decisions have consequences. It's a strange feeling to know that you're successful in so many ways but not the way you absolutely need to be to play at life. You can't call Delta and say, "Sooo, I can't afford that flight, but I've written this blog three times a week for two and a half years so how 'bout you just give it to me on account of I deserve it?"

Would I change anything? No. But will I now sacrifice what I wasn't willing to sacrifice before? Yes. I'm ready to make that choice now.

It's only a few months, I keep saying to people when they stare at me with *WTF-are-you-thinking??* faces. But it's not about the amount of time, the distance from Manhattan or even the fact that I'm about to revert back to my six-year-old sleeping situation (except even then I had my own room). For me this is about addressing a source of stress and holdback in my life with a solution.

First I had to say, *this is what I want to change*. Then I had to say, *this is what I'm willing to do to change it*. And on Friday morning and the many mornings following I'll have to say, *this is what I am doing, and this is why*.

Wish my family luck...

Ed Note: When I wrote this post I was avoiding fessing-up to the big goal behind the move home: an eventual move to L.A. I don't know if I was afraid to confess it to my current bosses or afraid to confess it to myself, but I held it back from my friends and family for those first few months of commuting until it become less of a, "what if?" and more of a, "when will I."

I will say that it's weird to read this post now because all I can see is everything I'm not saying. It feels like a half-truth. Yes, I was moving home to save money so that all of my options could be open, but the option I was most seriously considering was a move to L.A.

Hopefully there are few posts that are this honest and yet still hiding something so big, though I guess we won't know that until another five years in the future...

What You'll Learn At Your Five Year College Reunion
from 6/7/10

To say that my friends and I had been preparing for the Boston College 5-year since we left BC 5 years ago isn't an exaggeration. It is a momentous occasion. So momentous that some people flew to it from Chicago the day before their business school finals begin *aanndd* others drove to it from South Boston at 8:00AM just to be on campus the minute registration opened. The amount of g-mail chains it took to make these three days happen is downright embarrassing, and yet, we are not embarrassed.

We've missed each other. We've missed the place we called home for four years. But mostly, we've missed what was *so awesome* about college (that being everything), and the idea of spending even three short days back in some semblance of that bliss made us happy beyond words. What the actual weekend made us also starts with an H, but it ends with an *-ungover*. It's taken me roughly four days to recover from said hangover and attempt to finally write about what it is like to attend your first college reunion.

Here - with an attempt at not incriminating (most) people - is what I've got:

- NOT drinking seven nights a week (and eating late-night cafeteria food 40-50% of those nights) does wonders for one's general appearance.

- It is really, really nice to be able to say, "I am a lawyer" or, "I am a doctor," or, "I am a teacher," when people ask you what you've been up to for the past five years. "I work in media doing sort of branded-entertainment and integrated marketing projects and also do some writing on the site but am ultimately trying to..." - you get it.

- There is no age at which people will *stop* breaking into places you tell them they can't go. Just leave everything open. It'll be easier for everyone.

- Being limited to two nights of partying is *very* dangerous. As Pierson put it, "what saved us from the 2AM-5AM mistake every night of college was that you had to see everyone in class the next day..."

- If you make this announcement - *Attention everyone: the bar will be closing in 4 minutes* - you need to purchase enough booze for what will follow.

- It remains almost impossible to dance on the two inch, wooden arm of a couch and not fall off

- If your name is John Kennedy you are a God-of-a-man and excellent source of publicity for my writing. (How was that Kennedy?)

- Everyone knows everything about what everyone's been doing for the past five years because of Facebook. This makes it completely acceptable to say, "Hey! Looks like law school's been a blast! Sorry to see you're not dating that blonde guy you were with in all those pictures our first year out. Oh, and awesome pictures from your trip to India!" Or, at least, it got acceptable around midnight.

- Purchasing nips (airplane bottles for you non Boston-area college students) for consumption in transit from one activity to the next saves nights. It does the opposite to lives.

- Someone will *always* fall for the "no pants party" invite. Well played, T.K.

- And - and brace for over-sentimentality - if you work hard at keeping in touch with all the friends that made your college experience perfect, reunion isn't sad or awkward or depressing at all - it's just a three day re-live of the absolute time of your life.

Let the countdown to the 10-year begin.

Ed note: I am now less than two years away from my ten-year college reunion. My feelings regarding the arrival of this event are exactly the same as they were before the first time it went down. The only problem is that this time I'll be bringing a husband...who didn't go to Boston College. Let the Gmail chains begin!

My Busband And Me

from 7/12/10

I realize it's been weeks since I've updated on my suburban summer. It's not for lack of material. It's just that once I start in on a topic - no matter the direction - it somehow downward spirals into the conclusion that living a 1.5 hours bus-ride away from your entire existence *suuuucks*. And I try not to say sucks too much; it upsets my Mom.

But after ten weeks of commuting four hours a day, I am pleased to report that I've found the silver lining in my 5:15AM mornings, 10PM arrivals home, and I-currently-share-a-room-with-a-21-year-old existence His name is *either* Evan, Sam, Josh, or Jake (but *maaybe* also Bobby), but to me (slash my entire family) he is my *Bus-band*.

My Busband takes the Route 139 NJ Transit 55-seater from Freehold Mall to New York's Port Authority Bus Terminal ("The Poop"), just like me. We tend to hit the 6:53AM non-express piloted by either 75-year-old-Darryl-Hannah or Everyone's-10th-grade-geometry-teacher (so, Mr. Pendergast), but one Tuesday and two Fridays we enjoyed our respective home-brewed Dunkin French Vanillas in our respective (parents?) homes and perused the New York Times on our Mac laptops for just five more minutes before sauntering to make the 7:03AM. At least that's what I imagine he did because that's what I did, and in my imagination we're a match made in heaven.

My Busband and I have yet to speak (verbally), but I'm fairly certain he works in advertising, engineering, journalism or at a non-big-four accounting firm. This I've deduced from a combination of explicit clues and things I'm totally making up. For example: his style of dress.

It's business casual but with a tendency toward button downs and Ferragamo loafers (we'll get to those) versus polo shirts and/or dressy T's with boat shoes. Finance or major accounting firm, and he'd be in a suit or at the very least tie. Also, there is a bus that goes directly to Wall Street, which he's clearly opting against. I've determined this is either because he does not work anywhere near Wall Street *or* because he noticed my arrival at the Route 139 to The Poop while in line for the Route 325 to Wall Street and decided - *hell, I'll just take the subway.* Unclear.

So finance, good accounting firms and probably law are all out leaving us with the list of options I'm willing to allow for our life together: engineer/architect, journalism, and ad agency. As I see it, these professions attract the type I refer to (affectionately) as the Metro-Nerd. He has non-gelled hair but in a well-kept cut. He carries a newspaper, but the read-order goes Front Page *then* Sports. He has an iPhone or the latest Blackberry, but not a Kindle or Nook. This is a Metro-Nerd not Techno-sexual (Sorry. Couldn't help myself). It is worth noting that my Busband carries a fashionable male messenger bag (yes, Jack Spade), which does make both his sexuality and relationship status suspect *but* he drives an incredibly old Jeep Wrangler (soft top), which is not the car of a gay man or suburban fiancé (stereotypically speaking). And, I know, there are those pristine Ferragamo loafers, but they're black and he sometimes pairs them with outfits clearly requiring a brown shoe. No gay man would make that mistake, and no girlfriend would allow it to be made.

And so we go on - morning in and evening out - enduring this silent dance together. When he boards the bus before I, I saunter past his regular spot (left side, 6th row in, window position) with obviously purposeful non-direct eye contact. A sort of non-hello *hello* with an undertone of we're-in-this-together-but-not-like-I-call-you-my-Busband-or-anything-weird-like-that!

When I board the bus before he, I sit down in any row before the 6th row on the left side, aisle position, quickly whip out my iTouch and speed-scroll to Podcasts: *This American Life* with the screen ever-so-slightly-angled to the side so passers-by may see my intellectual en-route routine.

Do I long for the day when we might finally speak - a, "hm, the 6:53 is late today...wonder what the issue is?" or, "(yawn) Friday's are tough, huh? At least my media agency job allows me to wear jeans. You?" Yes, of course I do. Long, drawn-out processes for meeting mysterious potential husbands are kind of my forte. But do I really want to date this fellow Monmouth County money saver who's either on an identical campaign to bolster his Roth IRA (slash start one) or simply chooses to live 1.5 hours from his job slash life? No *way*. He's either makes too little money to afford to live in Manhattan, foolishly squandered away what he did make, necessitating the move home, or totally committed to life in Freehold, New Jersey.

Sadly, none of those situations are datable. I mean, do you *know* how much it *suuuucks* to commute four hours a day every single day?!

Ed Note: I never did speak to my Busband before leaving my commuting life for the big move to L.A., but I also never saw him get dropped off by a girlfriend figure in our time traveling together, so I can only assume that he had the same fake relationship with me that I had with him.

Several years later, my sister Dani started commuting the city on that same bus line. I asked her to look out for my Busband, but she said she never saw a man by the very specific description I provided. So maybe he finally saved enough for that apartment in the city, or maybe Dani was lying so she could steal my Busband for her own daily commuting fantasies. If so, I support her because nothing, I mean NOTHING sucks more than commuting to New York City on the 139 bus from Freehold Center.

jessie rosen

On Being The Mayor of a Non-Existent Town

from 8/2/10

Today I'm writing from The Land of 10,000 lakes, the birthplace of Target, and the state where – as my Meme here says – the mosquito is the official bird. To me it's always just been the place that explains why my Dad wears shorts in the house all winter long.

I am here for a difficult reason – the passing of my grandfather, Poppey – but in this family, mourning takes the shape of a multi-day storytelling session with breaks for food (if you call blintz soufflé food, which would be an insult to blintz soufflé). It's the kind of place at the kind of moment where an almost-27-year-old grappling with major life changes should be quarantined and given high doses of when-we-were-your-age stories intravenously. It's also a bizarrely fervent fan base for this blog meaning no story – wisdom-filled or otherwise – begins without "oh – I've got one! Now *this* one is for sure going to make the blog!" Correction: no story Uncle Evan starts.

I am a good audience for a good story (if you don't mind being misquoted), and owing to the IQ and long-term memory of this side of my family, there are countless tales to tell (*none* of which compare to the time Poppey took a solo ride on a Zoo elephant at the age of late-60-something because my cousin Sam chickened out on the elephant boarding dock. "Look! No Hands!"), but in story-shower situations I always become more interested in the patterns than the details. Maybe it's because being a writer gives you an ear for the overarching narrative that comes out of the events? Maybe it's because I'm more interested in who the character is than what they do? Whatever the reason, come story 10 of 10,000 (new state motto?), I go into what-would-we-title-thebiopic? mode. I listen for the thesis statements about the people in the stories. As the now-very-non-PC adage goes, were they chiefs? Were they Indians? Were they Mr. Potters or George Bailey's? If we're all just some form of the characters in *The Wizard Of Oz*, which part would they play?

With the stories of my Poppey both shared and gleamed in the short time since we've arrived in Minnie, I have my overarching narrative and with that, a lesson on how to live that can sometimes only be taught once you've stopped living. It's a life lesson I'd like to bottle and re-feed myself whenever the questions of how-should-I-behave-in-this-world comes up.

The lesson is that you can be an unelected mayor of a non-existent town without a day of campaigning and that, if you are able to achieve that kind of stature in that kind of no-boundaries community, it will define your life *and* the life of that community. It is also about how a couple (Poppey is Meme's counterpart, to complete the oddly-named set) can have a style of life so compatible that it's hard to determine which personality influenced the other.

See there are people who go to the grocery store to pick up a few things and people who go to the grocery store to visit with the owners, talk about the Twins game, and *then* pick up a few things. There are people who have a doctor they see when they are sick and people who have a doctor they call by first name, buy meaningful gifts, and speak of as if he's family. Some people go to a religious center for worship. Other people go to a religious center for community, friendship, education, and to workout with the congregation's fitness instructor who then becomes the kind of friend that visits the house upon their passing. Some people have children that they care for like parents care for children. Other people have those plus a gaggle of other people who somehow become *like* children. There are people who are sought out for advice and council because they have degrees in advice and council giving and there are people who are elevated to that kind

20-NOTHINGS

of oracle-stature because they know the right things to say.

They're not chiefs. They're not Indians. They're not even community leaders or elders. They're just people who on-purpose or because they can't help themselves – reach out and touch a community in a way that gives them an un-official, official role in their world. And as their life comes to an end, they are the very rare kind of people who receive a donation in their name from the owner of their favorite restaurant.

And those are just a few examples.

People will give you lots of advice on how to live your life. Big-picture advice about financials and religions and proper number of kids spaced a proper number of years apart. After my time here in America's heartland picking up advice on life-in-general based on the sad passing of one life-in-specific, I've gleamed that the big picture is made of the tiny actions that make you known in community you occupy - the tasks of a campaigning mayor who doesn't know he's campaigning and doesn't want to run any government.

They tell actresses to, "make the whole room remember you." I think the thesis statement of all the stories I've heard here is, remember every single person in the room, and they won't want to forget you.

Ed Note: One of the first things I noticed about R after we started dating were his mayor-like qualities. Well, it wasn't so much something I "noticed" as something that smacked me in the face in the form of Vito – the owner of Vito's pizza on La Cienega - giving me a bear hug and treating me to a free pie as he whispered, "she's a keeper, kid." R is of no relation to Vito. He is also of no relation to the couple who own Blue Note Dry Cleaners on Robertson, the doorman at Roger Room or Haru, owner of Haru Sushi Café.

jessie rosen

There are people who are most comfortable being anonymous and people who are most comfortable being known. I like to surround myself with the latter. It helps remind me that I aspire to be the latter. Apparently, it runs in the family.

I'm Officially My Scary Age

from 8/7/10

It's finally happening. I'm turning my scary age tomorrow. The terrifying 2-7.

Two years ago, when this whole scary age situation came about, I said there was a chance I'd adjust for inflation once the number arrived, but now that it's here I've decided it stays. Not because I am petrified to be turning 27, devastated that my early 20's are over, depressed about what's to come and other such Cathy Comic strip shit. It's not about that. It's about where this number falls in the arc of life and how that makes me feel about where I've been and where I'm going.

It's like Katie said in that original "Scary Age" post, "it's the point at which I feel like I really have to get my life together - like every decision from here on out has to be really deliberate, towards some kind of end life happiness."

I'm sure 30-year-olds are rolling their eyes at this decision, 35-year-olds are about to stop reading, and people my parents' age (if not my actual parents) are making that, "if you think 27 is scary..." face. They're all right and valid, but so am I.

In many, many ways these days, age is just a number. You can get married at 25 or 40 and still have a biological family. You can change your career every decade for your entire life. You can start your 30s in incredible debt and end them a millionaire. Martha Graham was a prima ballerina at 50-something and Doogie Howser was an M.D. at 15. Our options are limitless.

But that doesn't mean we don't *feel* a certain way about hitting certain numbers, and it doesn't mean we shouldn't pay attention to our pacing along the way. In my head there are things, career-wise, that I've always wanted to accomplish by the time I'm 30. If I get there without checking them off the list I won't be a failure, but that doesn't mean I shouldn't set goals and work to hit them. One of those things is to become a (legitimately) published author. 30 is a *very* young age to make that happen – I know and appreciate that – but if I don't draw a line in the sand, how am I supposed to stay motivated and prioritized? In the same way there are certain things, personal-things-wise, that I'd like to experience before I leave my 20s. One of those is to be in a long-ish term, committed relationship (so, longer than five months). That's not me saying I *have* to be married by 30. That's a goal because I think it is life enhancing to learn all the lessons that a committed relationship teaches while in your 20s. And so I look at myself at 27 and say, where have I been and what does that mean? What do I want, and how do I go about finding it?

27, to me, is that point at which you say, time to point the fun and games in a specific direction, time to take those major risks that you're in perfect shape to make happen, time to take stock or do an audit or whatever cliché works best and say, okay, good, but what if I just absolutely went for everything I really, truly desire?

But when I originally picked my scary number it was about that pit in your stomach you feel when you realize you forgot to take the perfect picture at a given event that's never going to happen again - that, *shit-I-missed-it* feeling. Now that I'm actually here at 27 things are no less scary, but in a totally unexpected turn of events I feel like I *want* to be scared.

I want to have that pressure of feeling like there are items to check off in my 20s. I'm excited about drawing lines in the sand and pacing to meet them. The whole idea of the gravity of this point in life is exhilarating. It's not my scary age because I suspect I'll find my first grey hair before I turn 2-8. It's about the fact that the number 2-7 charges me with a motivation to commit to my passions and dive at the risks those passions require.

So I'm scared, yes. But at 27 I'd rather be scared with a purpose than fearless without a cause. I like to think it's just the motivational emotion I'll need for the adventure that's to come in my 27th year.

But more on that next week…

Ed Note: I stand by the lofty thoughts in this post and I'm proud to say I mostly lived in their spirit. That said, I think 28 is a more appropriate scary age for those currently in their early 20s on account of inflation and the success of IVF treatments. Or, what's probably more appropriate is to not define a scary age at all and just life your life as you see fit. Though, what's the fun in that?

It's Time to Tell the Blog

from 8/14/10

"So when are you going to tell the blog?" Mike asked after I confirmed that the news was official.

I laughed because of the way he said it - to "tell the blog" – like I have to sit the Internet down for a *we-need-to-talk*.

My news isn't really what this blog is about, I told him.

But when I thought about it - about the whole, long story that precedes the new chapter I'm about to begin - I realized it all did come back to this blog. *All* of it. And for once, I'm not over-exaggerating.

The whole, long story begins with Matt Pierson-made-me-start-this-blog-against-my-will and ends with I'm-moving-to-Los-Angeles-on-September-1st-to-pursue-my-creative-pursuits.

I realize that reads like whiplash, but the plot points between that start and this "finish" do puzzle piece together into an actual picture. It's essentially a picture of a *Shoots and Ladders* board, but at least there's a path.

Separately the events that lead to my decision are random, coincidental, ridiculous, and unbelievable. They guest star a combo of the most likely players (my parents) and unlikely characters (Suze Orman?!). And they feature way less OCD planning than most random Tuesdays of my life.

But as I sat down to figure out how exactly I got from there to here - from starting a blog just to have a reason to write to moving clear across the country to pursue a career in writing - I can with absolute certainty pick out those moments that were the "sure signs"- or God winks, right Mom? - that I knew I had to follow even though I didn't know where they were going.

An early wink (slash punch) came from David who is as critical as they come and three times that when it comes to me. He told me I had something good going with this blog but I was wasting it by only writing every so often. "You need to commit to three days a week," he said, "or don't do it at all."

I listen to David (unless it has anything to do with relationships), so I wrote regularly from that day on, and he was right; it took my writing from a dabbling to a body of work.

Then Nora started reading and, like the born producer she is, saw television material in my 500-word rambles. I told her I had no idea what it took to develop a television show. She ignored me, and for the next six months we worked on a treatment that ended up in the hands of a production company who optioned this title and my life for television development.

It was around that same time that a name I hadn't seen in 10+ years dropped back into my life.

Kim Kaye was my colleague (?) in Brownie Troop 180 who randomly re-introduced herself as a fan of this blog and (God wink) the new co-founder of a Manhattan-based theater company. "We want you to write a one-act play for us," she told me over dirt-cheap Thai in the Theater District.
    "I don't know how to write a one-act play," I said.
"It's not hard," she told me.

Kim has a B.A. in creative writing with a concentration in theater. I Googled "how to write a one-act play."

Four months later my first one-act play was staged at an off-off

(off?) Broadway theater, and I knew my life would never be the same. Dramatic, I know, but my friend Paul told me, "some things require some drama, girl."

If you asked me when I was ten years old if I loved to write I would have said, yes. If you asked me if it was my passion - the thing I want to make a life out of - I would have asked what that means.

If you told me at 18, *hey, you should pursue writing for film and television*, I would have said, "Um, thank you," but thought, "Um, you're crazy." At 18 I still loved to write, but the idea of turning that hobby into that specific dream just wasn't in my frame of reference. The same goes for my college years when writing became even more a part of my life (the website friends and I launched, the college TV show we produced), but even then I felt like a girl who wrote, not a writer. There's a difference, and that difference is entirely mental.

Which is why I remember so distinctly the first time someone told me I was "a real writer." It was Blair Singer - a playwright who also spent some time writing on *Weeds* - and we were sitting down over beers at a bar in Brooklyn that looked just like a bar in Brooklyn would (Blair's line). I'd been set up with Blair to discuss him coming on board to supervise the potential *20-Nothings* TV show. Blair was far more interested in mentoring me to the point of being able to write it all myself. "I read your stuff," he told me, "and this is what you should be doing with your life."

That was the first time I thought, *I can do this*. I *want* to do this or, it would be *incredible* to be able to do this had come months before. I'd transitioned from developing-and-writing-content-is-a-dream to developing-and-writing-content-is-*my*-dream through the one-act play experience and my work with Nora, but I was stuck in that place so many people get stuck. "*I* can't do that. Come *on*. That's *crazy*."

But as if answering the in-my-head-objections with in-my-face interruptions you'd have to be an idiot to ignore, the universe said, "Yeah, it's crazy. Deal with it."

A middle school friend who'd landed at an LA talent agency came back into my life and helped me navigate that world, another friend put me in touch with an editor at The Daily Beast and then an editor at Marie Claire who assigned me articles that drew bigger attention, my theater company circle became a source of game-changing inspiration and lead to my writing The Hook-up Conversations, a full-length play. And then one incredible woman at one LA-based talent management company sent me an unsolicited e-mail that changed my life.

How's that for dramatic?

For the past ten months I've been working with Lucinda and the team at that management company to develop my writing portfolio to the point of pitching my own material for sale. I have also been working to develop my understanding of the previous sentence. And Lucinda, with tireless patience and fairy-godmother-like skill has been working on convincing me that this is real, I can do it, and making the move west is the best next step.

Which is where I'm-moving-to-Los-Angeles-on-September-1st comes in. Though, if you ask my mother, I'm not *moving* – I'm just, "going to live somewhere else for a little while," (apparently, we're all writers).

There comes a time in the exploration of any desire, dream or passion where you have to ask yourself, *how bad do I want it?* Bad enough to leave my current, *great* job? Bad enough to move away from the city I love more than any other place I've ever been? Bad enough to leave my family and some of my closest friends? Bad enough to risk failing?

Some of those answers are *yes*, but some of them are still *I don't know*, which explains why this decision comes ten and not two months after that e-mail from Lucinda.

But as I stepped slowly toward this final decision (and away from my attachment to Manhattan's 24-hour bodegas) I realized the more important question is, are you willing to *never* have it? Are you willing for it to *never* happen?

Yes, going for it means a whole list of things that make my stomach turn could happen, all of which are completely unknown. But not going for it leads to something I can absolutely guarantee – it won't happen.

There's an Anaïs Nin quote that I've always loved: "And the day came when the risk to remain tight in a bud was more painful than the risk it took to blossom."

And so I'm going to LA (in three weeks, gulp), and I'm absolutely certain it's the right thing for me to do.

I have much more to say about this decision, about what it means to be a 27-year-old woman making this change, about the lessons in this story that we can all stand to play on repeat, and – most importantly – about the people who have made this possible for me, but for right now I'll leave it at the story of how it came to be.

In one sentence: I'm a very lucky girl blessed with very loving mentors who pushed me through all the open doors so I could make the decision to walk through this big one.

I can't promise that I'm fully ready for what's next or sure of what I even want in the end, but I will promise you this - the blog is going no where.

Ed Note: This is my favorite Ed Note to write because nothing went as I planned when I moved to L.A. – career-wise at least. My hair did become far less frizzy and I stopped wearing a ton of black, so that worked out.

That manager who encouraged me to move left the business the week I arrived. Yes, you read that correctly. Almost a year later I finally signed with a new manager. Six months after we started working together, she also left the business. It took another full year for me to find the managers who currently represent me, and they own their own company so I'm fairly hopeful they won't close up shop without a good deal of notice.

It took almost two and a half years after the day I moved for me to leave the full-time job I moved with – an awesome job in branded content production – and become a full-time writer. In other words, I did not move to L.A. and become a writer the minute I stepped onto Hollywood soil. And yet, every day I spent here got me closer to that goal.

So to conclude the Public Service Announcement that is this post – it takes time, but every single step is a step toward the goal. In which case, you may as well start today.

It's Not You, Armin. It's My Brand New, Overwhelming Life

from 9/10/10

This morning I lied over the phone to a man I've never met at the Volkswagen dealership in Van Nuys, California. His name was Armin. Well - *is* Armin but I've never met him and never will, so to me he no longer exists.

Armin and I met over my e-negotiations for a Jetta lease. Per Greg's advice, I spent the days since arriving in L.A. contacting various VW dealerships for Jetta quotes, pitting those quotes against each other and negotiating my price down from one number with zero relevance what-so-ever to me to one considerably smaller number with slightly more relevance now that an installment of it has been removed from my bank account.

Armin had been the front-runner early on. He came in low, piled on the extras, and told me moving to L.A. was the best decision I've ever made. He validated my want to go *salsa* red vs. black, and when I said, "I know it's frivolous, but I really want a moon roof he said, "You're in L.A. You *need* it, and it's *sun* roof." Armin was the angel at the gate between SoCal heaven and me. As such, I had every intention of finalizing my deal in Van Nuys so I could finally return the terrifying Jeep Grand Cherokee I'm borrowing from family friends and get on with my new, red-themed life.

…Until I got an email from Michael at Volkswagen of Santa Monica that beat Armin's offer and promised a blue tooth hook-up.

"But Armin was so nice!" I said to Mike.

"Are you aware of how far Van Nuys is?" he said back.

And so I closed the deal in Santa Monica and started screening Armin's calls. Making the right decision was hard enough. Explaining that decision to a lovely man who had been among the nicest of my L.A. life thus far was too much. Maybe this is because disappointing people is my most hated emotion? Do you *remember* how much it stung when Mom or Dad said, "I'm not mad...I'm...disa*ppointed...*" Or maybe it's because this week has been so filled with emotional decision after emotional decision that I'm emotionally, decisionally tapped out.

I told Armin I went with a Honda Civic from the dealership of a family friend.

Yep. That lame. The car-lease equivalent of "it's not you, it's me" or "I've actually started talking to my ex-boyfriend back home again." A bold-faced lie (over the phone...).

The logical, no-emotional-strings-attached response would have been, "I got a better offer, and I want to buy a car in Santa Monica." Simple. Honest. True.

Just as simple as, "I'm sorry, but it just isn't working out between us," or, "I met someone else," or even, "I don't think we make compatible friends," or, "I've found a different job and will be leaving the company," or, "I can't come to your birthday party because one of my better friends is having one that same night."

Stripped of all the feelings, the simple facts are facts, and they hold up just as well, if not better, than the lie. But when we get wrapped up and connected in the people on the other end of those statements, it isn't cut and dry.

After the car purchase, I think I'm officially done making major, emotional life choices. But, just in case, I've decided to secure the remainder of my bedroom decor items online. Fedex employees don't care that the grey satin comforter was just a little too satin-y, but you're really sorry because it's such a lovely comforter and you fully intend to purchase a *different* Anthropologie comforter instead.

Ed Note: Every single month when I pay my lower-than-Armin-could-offer-me car bill, I think back on this moment and both pat myself on the back for securely an incredibly low monthly car bill then kick myself in the ass for lying to a perfectly kind stranger. Just kidding. I hadn't thought about Armin since the day I wrote this post, almost three years ago.

Though, in September of this year my current lease will be up, and I'm now wondering if it makes sense from a karma perspective to go get my second car from Armin. You think he'll remember me, right? I mean how many people go to lease a Jetta and, "end up with a Honda Civic?"

California Culture Shock

from 9/22/10

I have lived in LA for 2.5 weeks, but it still feels like I'm on some weird vacation - like my car is a rental car that I don't *really* have to worry about, like I should do as much as humanely possible in a given day because I only have so many left, like I can wear white jeans even though it's essentially October...

I can't quite explain the all-consuming feeling of being totally off-kilter after the transition from New York City to the suburb that is Los Angeles (sorry, but this is not a city) but like I told Zac yesterday on Gchat, it's as if I'm a goldfish whose water's just been changed so I'm all swimming around seizure-style in no particular direction, forgetting things after two minutes and mistaking tiny pieces of grain for food (dramatic, yes, but people do eat less here). Also my jewelry is all still in boxes and my hanging clothes are out of color/style order (ROYGBIV, shirts/skirts/dresses/pants, obvs), so I can't focus on a damn thing. You know how it is.

Still, in vacation slash gold fish-interrupted mode, my perception of all that is new/different/oh-so-LA is razor sharp. Here's what I've got after 2.5 weeks:

- There is a food truck here called the NomNom truck. I don't know what they sell out of said truck, but I don't care. I will eat it as soon as possible and report back. If this pertains to you specifically, you get it.

- Every day I learn a new industry phrase/jargon/term. My favorite so far is "to give good meeting" as in, "her ideas are *meh*, but she gives really good meeting." Yeah, I know...

- I am more dressed up than anyone I encounter at any place I go. Today someone at my office literally said to me, "wow, that's an actual outfit." I responded, "Yep, I like clothes" (gold-fish-brain mode), but I thought, "Um, no it's not. I'm clearly not accessorizing to my full potential because my necklaces are still in boxes. How could you not SEE that?!!"

- People in L.A. are completely immune to several of the things I find most shocking about this town: traffic, the weather, and the cost of valet parking. I believe it's a learned defense mechanism, like how when you bring up how bad New York smells in the summer, people pretend they don't notice.

- A surprising number of people I'm meeting went to Ivy League schools, which is great cause it's always good to have very smart people around, but it's kind of like, shouldn't you all be curing cancer and solving whatever goes down in the Middle East instead of coming up with phrases like "gives good meeting"???

- The kind of things you see people do alone in their cars is *amazing*. Today I passed a girl who appeared to be applying fake eyelashes at a stoplight on Olympic and Doheney (those are two palm-tree-lined streets where very famous things happens, obvs). Also, because everyone has blue tooth in their cars, you constantly see people carrying on full conversations with no one, windows *wiiiide* open. Yesterday I heard a woman say, "You can $!*#@ me seven ways 'til Sunday if you just replace the god-damned light bulb in the nanny's room. She can't READ at night. And if she can't READ at night she's in a piss poor mood all day. And I won't have our kids raised by a moody nanny." I'm not paraphrasing.

- The breakfast burrito is to Los Angeles what the bagel with cream cheese and lox is to New York. As such, I'm on a campaign to eat every single one available. So far I'm at six, and I've only been here for four brunches.

- A pool party is to Los Angeles what a roof party in to New York. This is great because pools are fun and a lot cooler than roofs (rooves?). This is bad because you wear significantly less clothing to a pool.

- I've learned that it's not technically name-dropping if you really do know the person and hang out with them. Name-dropping would be me being like, "I was at this Newline thing with Leonardo DiCaprio the other night. Party was lame, but they had it catered by the NomNom food truck." Whereas completely legitimate L.A. conversation would be: "Leo was in the office last Thursday for a pitch around this new concept for HBO. We ordered in from the NomNom truck because that's his favorite."

- If you were or currently are an assistant in any other city in the world and you think you worked really, really hard, you're wrong. The Los Angeles assistant is second to nothing. They make things happen with two blackberries, a landline and Microsoft Outlook that would wow that guy who built the Iron Man suit. Because of this, I am very seriously considering changing my selection for stranded on a desert island companion.

Ed Note: I have now lived in Los Angeles for almost three years (or 156 weeks), and all these observations stand I just now find them completely and totally normal. Here are a few other things to which I've become completely immune:

- *If you arrive to brunch after 10:30AM it will be crowded because you're late. Brunch starts at 10AM, or 9:30 if you hiked Runyon that morning.*

- *Going to more then one bar in one night is considered aggressive.*

- *You could give two craps about the fact that you're seeing a celebrity if said celebrity is taking up one of the precious seats at the coffee shop where you write.*

- *The Farmer's Market is a legitimate social scene. Like people say, "want to meet at the Farmer's Market on Sunday?" and they mean that as a get-together.*

- *60 degrees is cold.*

Surviving the First Mini Trip as a Couple

from 11/22/10

Now seems like as bad a time as any to expose the fact that I'm a fraud.

For the past three years I've written a blog focused in large part on dating and relationships while remaining pretty much single and very much inexperienced in the realm of life as a couple. Up until three weeks ago I hadn't dated someone long enough to meet the parents. Not since high school have I purchased a birthday gift for a man I call boyfriend. And never have I ever played the female part in a couple's Halloween costume (*or* the male!).

So when the idea for R and me to get out of L.A. for a weekend came up, I was slightly more than slightly panicked. And when I was later informed that the idea has, in fact, been mine, I about fell over.

"Well since you claim this was my idea," I told the most patient 28-year-old man this side of the Mississippi, "can I change it from two nights to one?"

And so we left this past Saturday morning for Ojai, California (not just the name of the family business in ABC's now defunct hit, *Brothers & Sisters*!). R had taken care of absolutely everything like some living, breathing 36-hours in _____ New York Times article leaving me plenty of time to over-think every element of our uninterrupted alone time together.

Do not get me wrong, I very, very much like R and was very, very much excited for our maiden voyage together. But that in no way prevented me from being preoccupied with fear about the myriad things that could go wrong. I am a mental multi-tasker.

My fears included but were not limited to:

- Getting carsick on the ride up. No, I don't generally get car sick, but every once in awhile I'll look down at my phone too much while passenging and start to feel a little wonky. This is embarrassing because it doesn't slash shouldn't happen to people over the age of eight.

- Absolutely hating the way R drives on the freeway and questioning the quality of his entire person as a result of this finding.

- Not really remembering how to ride a bike. I've gone five plus years without riding a bike and found that, despite what they say, it is not just like riding a bike. This one's doubly problematic because I can't possibly look adorable in a bike helmet and therefore run the risk of suffering a massive head injury resulting from my inability to remember how to ride a bike and vainly refusing to wear a helmet. (Note: We didn't end up biking but did go on a "hike" during which I wore a Louis Vuitton saddle bag and carried a large, skim cafe au lait.)

- Finding out that we are wildly indecisive as a couple in situations that require "winging it." *R: So we have an hour to kill, what should we do? Me: I don't know...what do you want to do? R: I want to do what you want to do. Me: Well I don't know what I want to do!*

- Finding out that we are wildly incompatible as a couple in situations that require "winging it" *R: So we have an hour to kill. What do you want to do? Me: I'd like to spend 15 minutes in each of the seven vintage clothing stores in town. You? R: I'd like to drive around and see if we can find somewhere to shoot skeet. Also, fifteen minutes times seven is more than sixty. Me: Oh, and ew.*

- Talking in my sleep, snoring, and/or passing gas in the night (slash at any point over the course of the trip). If these fears were placed in order of gravity, this would be #1. If you are reading this and thinking, *what's the big deal?*, you are probably a man. If you are reading this and thinking, *um, one or more of those did happen*, and you want to stay my boyfriend, keep it to yourself.

None of the above happened (I repeat: if you know otherwise, zip it). It was, in fact, just as comfortable slash fun as spending 36 hours together here in L.A. except we've never gotten involved in a competitive wine taste-off here and don't generally see barefoot pregnant women dancing to a band of four, 65-year-old men performing a set that 180'd from a Credence medley to an Incubus hit.

Maybe this relationship stuff isn't as complicated as I've made it out to be over 500 posts in the three years of writing this blog.

"Yeah, I've been meaning to talk to you about that," R said as he lowered the Ojai playlist he made us for the ride there and back (I know...), "I did some back-reading of the blog. I think you might have be over-thinking some things."

Forgot one:

- That my boyfriend will start reading old blog posts and realize just how insane I am.

Ed Note: R and I have since been on at least a dozen mini trips since this first voyage. We continue to find ourselves compatible in all elements of vacations, I continue to sometimes get car sick, and I R continues to pretend that I don't snore when I'm drunk. Regarding the ability to ride a bike: I've successfully avoided it thus far.

My Car Battery and My Status as a Woman

from 1/31/11

Last week my car battery died, and I decided that it's okay to need a man in your life.

I promise the rest of this post will be less dramatic, but not by a lot.

It was a Thursday night, and R and I were on our way back from Thousand Oaks, California where we'd gone to see my good friend Paul in his performance with the touring company of A Chorus Line. I was *!!!!!!* about it. R was *!!* about my being *!!!!!* about it. How R actually felt about seeing B-level Broadway on a weeknight would and will remain a total mystery. This is one of R's finest and most appreciated qualities.

There are a lot of details that are significant about this part of the story, but I'll spare you most of them. Just know that Thousand Oaks, California is 30-some-odd miles from L.A. and 50-some-odd miles from Santa Monica, where both R and I were prior to departing for the show. It took 1.75 hours to travel those 50-some-odd miles. We went to dinner before the show at a restaurant called Exotic Thai where we ate one Chinese and two Japanese dishes. After the show we took my friend Paul for a celebratory drink at the one venue open past 10PM - a BJ's. BJ's has an incredible dessert called the Pizookie, which is a hot cookie topped with ice cream. R had a really bad cold. And, upon arriving home to L.A. at 12:30AM, my car battery was dead.

There are a lot of details that are significant to my car battery being dead, but I'll spare you all of them because I have absolutely no idea how it happened, when it happened, or if it's going to happen again. Just know that car issues of any kind are among my greatest fears and frustrations, and that it was probably my fault. I've never had my own car; I've never wanted my own car, and most days I contemplate abandoning the one I have and spending the monthly lease fee plus insurance and gas on a personal driver. Unfortunately I've looked into the costs for that sort of thing and they're slightly higher than the lease on 2010 Jetta, despite the leather interior and sunroof. Total injustice.

Needless to say, I am beside myself upon finding out that the battery is dead. I'm concerned, confused, tired, annoyed, Pizookie-stuffed, and convinced that my street is a danger-ridden place, my car is a total lemon, and that I've already caught R's cold.

There are many difficult life scenarios in which I perform well to very well. I'm incredibly comforting at a funeral. I know how to mediate a group of sisters who can't remember what they're fighting about. If you're a sexually confused man looking to decide whether you belong in or out of the closet, I'm your girl (and it's out). But throw me into a scenario in which I must perform a technical task related to heavy machinery for which I am financially responsible, and I will crumble. Put that task on a dark street at a late hour with a man who just wants to help, and I will add a layer of stubborn anger to that crumble that would scare a AAA man away.

"What's the problem?" R kept saying, "I'm here. I have jumper cables. I know what to do with them. No one's going to bother us. I'm going to teach you how to jump the car and charge the battery so you won't have any problems in the morning. It'll take 15 minutes, tops."

He does not yet know that no amount of logic works on my in this scenario.

See, in this scenario, an independent feminist is waging war against girl who's learning to be in a relationship in my mind. I should know how to jump a car, and I should have an AAA card in case I don't. I'm now a needy, typical keep-you-up-'til-1AM-making-your-bad-cold-worse girlfriend who's as helpless as they come. (I warned you about the level of drama...).

No, this doesn't make sense, and I know that. There are plenty of men out there who wouldn't know what the hell to do, but the man I'm standing with does, and he's saying things like, "I'm so glad I'm here so I can teach you how to do this," and, "If I wasn't here I would expect you to call me to come over here and help you." I'm making weird whining noises and a face that says both, "thank you," and, "there goes my independence!" (jaw structure is similar to "pathetic").

We jumped the car. We got in and drove together around the block for five minute so my battery would re-charge. We re-parked the car in a safe spot with ample room in front and back in case (as I suspected) a parallel parker bumped it and the alarm went off all day draining the battery. And then I made R quiz me on how to do the whole thing all over again so I could do it on my own next time.

I cannot explain why taking kind and patient help with something I know nothing about makes me feel like less of a woman slash person. Maybe it's because I feel most natural being the more helpful and able party in a party of two? Because my self-confidence is rooted in self-preservation? Because my mind still exists in single girl mode? Maybe it's because I'm inclined to want what each person gives in a relationship to be totally equal so that it's really more like the best high school group project you've ever worked on?

Or maybe it's because in that moment I realized that I *looooved* having a guy around to make it all better, and that made me feel part guilty, part nervous and totally unlike myself...

Whatever it was - the source of my ridiculous neurosis - I got over it. I took the help, I liked the help, and I didn't do what I was inclined to do which was buy R some over-the-top thank you gift for providing the help.

...and then, *dying* though I was to buy my very own jumper cables to keep in my own car to fix my own messes, I didn't. Instead I just haven't given R his back. Baby steps.

Ed Note: I am pleased to report that I have not had to jump a car since that incident, however I do keep jumper cable in my trunk just in case. And, as if re-paying R for his patience on that late-night several years ago, we recently used those cables to help an old lady stranded on our street, and she ended up being the mother of the president of Viacom (MTV, Vh1, Comedy Central etc.), and she repaid us by setting R up on a meeting with her son. It all comes full circle.

The Long Overdue Story of How R and I Met

from 2/14/11

>**Me:** "I'm not trying to *hide* you from the Internet. It's just that my blog isn't about every detail of my romantic life. I'm a very private person!"
>**R:** "Fine. All I'm trying to say is that I think the people want more R, Jess."

And so, in a spirit of today-is-Valentine's-Day, here it finally is - the story of how I met R - whose name is technically Robby, but I think we'll stick with R.

Sometime last April I received an unexpected Facebook message from a college friend who I'd kept in loose contact with over the years since graduation. Let's call her C. C is a fantastic girl, and our friend groups were always intertwined, but I was surprised to read what the message said:

Listen, I'm not sure if you're seeing anyone, or if you want to be, and I'm sorry if this is a little bold of me, but I have this friend in L.A. that I think you'd really like, so let me know the next time you're on the west coast for work and I'll introduce you two. Who knows, could make for a fun cross-country romance.

There are people you expect to set you up - a family member, a roommate, a co-worker - and people you don't. It's not that I didn't think C could identify a good guy for me, I just didn't think I was on her radar of people to yenta.

Apparently, the way she explained it, I wasn't. "I don't know how it popped into my head," C told me months after," I had just seen him, and then I was reading your blog, and it just clicked." (In her honor I've since committed to spending less time thinking of outfits and more time thinking of others).

At the time, I lived in New York (as did C) but was making trips to L.A. for work, though C friend didn't know that. She also didn't know that I was very seriously considering moving to L.A. and had already begun the process of finding work out there. And C had no idea that I was planning my next trip when she sent the message, that it was less than a month away *and* that she would *also* be in L.A. that same week. It was too many coincidences for even a cynic to ignore.

It wasn't until months after we met that I found out C had barely mentioned me to R before I joined them for a drink in L.A. at The Darkroom. I assumed he'd been prepped to turn on the charm and make a good impression.

> **R:** "I didn't know anything about you," R later told me, "Why? Did you know a lot about me?"
> **Me:** Well, only what I could get off a minimally invasive Facebook stalk and fairly dead-end Google search."
> **R:** "You Googled me? Ha. That's so cool."

Apparently all C had said to R was, "there's going to be this girl Jessie there who you might like," which was smart because I then realized his behavior toward me was genuine (something to think about when setting people up in the future...).

In hindsight, it's too easy to say that we hit it off right away, so I'll just say that I was immediately drawn to him and we spent the rest of the night talking about all those first-date things that you forget immediately and have to awkwardly re-learn throughout the relationship. We were there for three, maybe four hours? And yes, there was kissing.

> **R:** "And you have to tell them about the juke box."
> **Me:** "What about it?"

> R: "About how we went to the juke box and picked songs together, and that's when we really knew we liked each other."
> Me: "I'm not going to tell them that! That's sooo cheesy."
> R: "No it's not, it's romantic. Just tell them. They'll love it."

Please see above (blush).

That was the first night of my week-long trip to L.A. R made a point to take me out on a proper date another night that week, and things went just as well as they had the night we met.

But again, I lived in New York, so my thoughts of what could become of this cross-country romance were minimal. I didn't know which end was up at the time, and the last thing on my mind was starting a long-distance relationship after 1.5 dates.

> R: "Yeah but I knew it would work out eventually."
> Me: "What?! How could you have known? We barely knew each other."
> R: "I had a good feeling about it."

It was that bizarre yet quiet confidence that I was so attracted to as we got to know each other over phone calls, e-mails, and games of Scrabulous. We didn't have the chance to get drunk and make stupid early-on dating mistakes. There wasn't the awkwardness of having to manage the hooking up versus really dating thing. We just slowly got to know each other.

R's family is from NJ/NY so he came east that 4th of July, and we fit in a NYC date. I went back to L.A. in August to make more progress on my potential move, and we saw more of each other then.

> R: "You forgot the part about the flowers."
> Me: "I'm not including that on purpose."
> R: "Come on. That was my best move!"

...And on that in August trip, R surprised me with the wildly impressive move of arranging for an insane bouquet of flowers to be waiting for me in the hotel where I was staying. Note included. That's when *I* had a feeling things were going to work out.

R came east again in August for an annual high school reunion that happened to fall on the week of my birthday, so he was there for the celebration. And by then I finally got a job in L.A. and decided it was time to make the move.

Now here's the part that R does not enjoy.

I did not intend to move to L.A. with a boyfriend. I was going through a major, major life change that had me in a total tailspin. I'd just left my entire family three thousand miles away. I was switching careers from something stable to something totally unknown. And, and this is his least favorite part, I was planning to play the L.A. field. I write a blog about it for crying out loud! How could I move to a brand new city and totally check myself out of the dating game?

I didn't put R on the back burner when I got to town, but I was very careful about the amount of time we were spending together those first few weeks. I am a commitment-phobe with a dangerously fierce sense of independence. I wasn't about to let a guy define my great, L.A. adventure.

> **R:** "I knew what was up."
> **Me:** "You did not! I had you shaking in your boots."
> **R:** "Nah. I told you. I knew it would be fine."

The rest is a strangely uncomplicated story for a girl who specializes in complicated stories. I loved being with him, he seemed to love being with me, and so we kept making plans, going on dates, and introducing each other to our individual groups of friends. I tried to keep the level of time spent together reasonable, but it got to the point where it felt ridiculous to deny something that felt more right than any dating situation had before.

> **R:** "That's because I mastered the slow play."
> **Me:** "Does the slow play involve wearing your heart on your sleeve and building all my IKEA furniture?"
> **R:** "*Allll* part of it, J."

We made it official in early October, the night of my housewarming party.

> **Me:** "I think you just tricked me into being your girlfriend."
> **R:** "SSsshhhh, let's just savor the moment."

The rest is still a very brief history that I am not embarrassed to call among the greatest surprises of my life. I'll spare you the details of what makes what we have work, but I will say that a big part of it is how hard we're both trying to take care of each other and how little effort it actually takes.

> **Me:** "Do you know what I really thought when I was trying to figure out what to do about you?" I said to R the other day.
> **R:** "That you'd never find someone this funny?"
> **Me:** "Still no. I thought, if I don't give this a go then someone else might get him, and I'm not willing to take that risk."
> **R:** "Wow. Look at you."
> **Me:** "I know. I've come a long way haven't I?"
> **R:** "Yeah, but I told you it would work out from the beginning."
> **Me:** "Ugh yo always say that! How were you so sure?!?"
> **R:** "I don't know. I just was."

And there you have it.

This year I think I'll spend Valentine's Day being grateful that I got out of my own way and into something wonderful.

Ed Note: I felt like R deserved the chance to support or refute the details contained with in this post. Also, considering how many times I've put words in the blog version of his mouth, you should hear him finally speak for himself, completely unedited, I promise.

"Even though we've retold this story countless times, especially since being engaged, I'm still amazed at how much "the story of us" is truly the story of us. The personality quirks, how we felt during the different stages of courting (I have no idea what other term to use), even the serendipitous plot points feel like things that defined the couple we are. The part of this story that you don't read in this blog post is my side of what happened. Not in a bad way of course, it's Jessie's blog after all. However, my side is fairly simple: when you meet someone you instantly connect to, you do things to keep that connection alive. You do the small things like calling her as she sat on the bus on her way home from Manhattan to the bigger things like surprising her with flowers. And you do it all because you want to, not out of obligation or trying to win her over by following some rules. As I hung out with Jessie more and more those first few months, what I fell in love first and foremost was her personality. All the honesty, trepidation, humor and caring you read in the blog is real. I'm guessing that's why you come back. And so did I. When people ask me "What would happen if Jessie didn't move to Los Angeles?" my answer is "I truly don't know but I'm glad I don't have to think about it." I'm excited to see where the story of us goes."

It Happened. I Become the Kind of Girlfriend I Hate.

from 5/19/11

I used to take pride in the fact that I wasn't a crazy, obsessive, nagging girlfriend. I was a go-with-the-flow girl, the kind that lets her boyfriend be who he is, live like he wants and dress as he pleases. I'd never remove a poster from a bedroom wall, criticize the way he cooks pasta or make him wear less baggy shorts that don't have mini stains on them.

Then I got a boyfriend who wore super baggy shorts with lots mini stains on them.

As I've made clear in previous posts that bear his letter, R is a wonderful man who leads a life in which I rarely find things to judge (and trust me, I can find a needle of judgment material in a haystack of perfection). So I was pleased to see that my in-going position on the kind of girlfriend I would be was coming true as a result of the kind of guy I had chosen.

Then shorts season hit L.A. (note: even though it's warm here all the time people follow general season attire because they really want to pretend they have seasons. It's weird.).

To backpedal yet again, R has very nice clothing. He isn't colorblind and generally knows what fits him. So shorts-gate was not the straw that broke this clothing horses' back. My request for R to buy all new summer shorts came out of a place of love, respect, and many years spent with gay best friends who wear much shorter shorts.

I wanted him to look nice. I wanted him to be stain free. And my understanding of what short-length is appropriate for a man has been, shall we say, skewed.

R was not thrilled. His old shorts are comfy and barely worn and the stains will come out with a little Shout spray, he claimed.

No, I said. They've got to go. They're way too baggy, do nothing for your legs and those are grease stains, they're not coming out.

The worst part is, I didn't feel bad about it right away. I felt like I'd triumphed over the forces of the former frat-boy. He would look great, and it would be my doing! When people saw us together they'd say, "who is that appropriate shorts-clad stud Jessie found, and can he talk to my boyfriend about the benefits of above-the-knee action?"

It wasn't until I found R wearing the old shorts, curtly asked why he insisted upon looking like a preppy rap star and was told that the shorts I made him buy are *weenie* that I realized I'd gone to that place I promised myself I'd never go.

Fine. It wasn't until I told him to stop complaining and go change then saw him fidgeting in the short shorts five hours later that I realized it.

Later than night I apologized: "I'm so sorry I turned into a nagging girlfriend who made you wear shorts you hate. I just want you to look nice, and I think the old shorts are a little tattered, and, and, and..."

R cut me off: "Are you seriously concerned about this?" he said. A question like that represents those tricky relationship moments where you have to tell the truth because it will be obvious if you don't despite the fact that lying is undoubtedly the better option.

"Yes," I said, "I really feel bad."

R laughed in my face and told me he doesn't hate the shorts and appreciates that I want to help him look nice. "But they're still weenie shorts," he said.

"Stop! It makes me feel bad when you say that!" I said.

"Too bad," he said.

And with that I think we may have both won.

Ed Note: R continues to refer to the shorts he now wears in several colors as weenie shorts, but mostly for my amusement. I am also pleased to report that on a recent shorts shopping trip he grabbed a new pair off the rack at the Banana Republic and said, "these are the kind I wear now, right?" I was about to say, "Only if those are the kind you want to," but instead I just said, "yes."

Graduating From College for the Third Time

from 5/25/11

I may or may not have mentioned that two of my younger sisters followed in my footsteps by attending the Boston College. This is very wonderful because we share the unique experience of knowing what it is to spend four years on "The Heights" learning to be "women and men for others" educated to "set the world aflame" (read: we have the same fifteen t-shirts and an unhealthy obsession with Jesuits). This is a total pain in the ass because it means I have had to endure the uniquely miserable experience of graduating from Boston College not one but *three* times.

SIX (my hands literally shook typing that number) years ago I graduated on a 45-degree, late May day as Boston's infamous "wintry mix" sloshed down on my poor family. I then proceeded to cry my eyes out for the four hours we were given to move out of my Gabelli Hall dorm while my parents packed the belongings I'd decided not to pack before their arrival. They still refer to it as the worst behavior of my entire life. "You were the meanest you've ever been on that day," my Mom says.

I cried because it was the end of the most special time I'd experienced to date. A phase of my life was dying, and I was in deep, uncontrollable mourning. I was terrified of the unknown to come, overwhelmed by the journey it had taken to get there and exhausted from the sleepless, drunk nights that preceded the big event.

I had both a conscious and unconscious knowledge of what it meant to be crossing over into this next phase of my life – adulthood – and what I knew is that I didn't want any part of it.

Four years after that, my sister Dani graduated on a 52-degree, late May day under cloudy skies that turned into a total downpour in the middle of her ceremony. I then proceeded to hide my half-dozen mini sob sessions for the far fewer hours it took to move her out of her Mod while her friends begged me for advice about when it was going to get less devastating (and their parents' asked when they were going to stop being such assholes).

I cried because I knew exactly what my sister was going through, how painful it was and the sad fact that it wasn't getting better particularly soon. I had the perspective of having seen some "success" in the "real world." I was doing the whole "adult" thing, and it was going fairly well, but being back in that moment still filled me with all this crazy emotion. Was I doing it right? Was I becoming the person I intended when I left this place? Was there any way to take a pause, rewind, move into a dorm-style apartment with my five best friends and re-train us to drink like fish without the risk of hangover? In other words, I cried for her but I was really still crying for myself.

Monday morning my sister Sara graduated on a 56-degree, late May day under skies that went from pouring to threatening to pour again all day long. (I guess the silver lining is that none of us can brag about our superior weather?) And after that, the strangest thing happened. I controlled myself and my tears for the fifteen minutes it took us to carry the neatly organized piles of things she'd prepared before our arrival (they call her "Best Rosen" for a reason).

Don't get me wrong, I was just as sad for Sara as I'd been for Dani and myself. I don't think the moment is any less devastating or worthy of misery. This time, though, my perspective on the event was totally...adult? I kept having these moments where I empathized with my parents and their pride/joy/sadness at their little girl accomplishing this major goal. On more than one bizarre occasion I looked around and thought about how I would be handling this if I were a parent. I think I actually hugged one of Sara's friends and said, "It's okay sweetheart. Being an adult is an incredibly exciting thing."

Maybe it was just a passing phase on a day when I was excited more excited about my future than sad about missing the past? Maybe I now know that there is some semblance of life after college (even if I can't guarantee that it starts anytime after the day you graduate)? Or maybe it's as simple as the fact that three's a charm when it comes to handling BC graduations.

Ed Note: In two years my littlest sister, Alex, will graduate from The University of Delaware. I will be a married 31-year-old, TEN YEARS out of college. I can currently bring myself to tears just thinking about attending this event. Yes, it will be because Alex Rosen, the baby of the family, is stepping into life as an adult, but it will also be because I will have spent double the amount of time out of college as I did in college. Turns out that three is not a charm when it comes to graduations of any kind. Thank god this will be my last...until I have kids of my own. I'll have to be drugged for those.

Letting My Freak Flag Fly: Suitcase Edition

from 6/17/11

I am currently on the East coast with R as his +1 to the wedding of one of his very best friends. It's taken me 27.9 years, but I am finally attending a wedding with a boyfriend. In negative news, I'm down one *killer* "never have I ever."

Naturally this kind of event comes with its stresses. I'm meeting some of R's best friends for the very first time, R's parents are also attending the wedding, and R and I are traveling clear across the country for three, jam-packed days of activity during which I'll have to drink, dance and stay awake. The number of costume changes required for this set of events numbers five, one of which is a bathing suit...that R's parents may or may not see me in. Also, I have no idea what late June in upstate New York feels like anymore.

All of that said, I had it under control. I was confident in my packing strategy and outfit decisions. I had recently tested pacing myself with vodka-only consumption at a dance party (with excellent results). And I just got one of those rod-only curling irons to achieve perfect, Kim Kardashian waves. I owned this wedding.

Untiiiil R made a suggestion that sent my T-minus-one-week-until-the-wedding prep into a tizzy:

- R: I have to check my golf clubs, so since I have to wait for baggage anyway, why don't we just pack in one, big suitcase instead of lugging our stuff around in two, separate carry-on's.

- Me: We pack our things together in one suitcase?

- R: Yeah. My black suitcase is huge. We can just...wait...why are you looking at me like that?....what's going on?...Oh no...I know that face...I said something really wrong...what is it?

What goes on inside the suitcase of a lady dressing for five events in three days taking place clear across the country is not a pretty thing. I'm a contained packer and a smart packer, but I am not the kind of packer I want other people reviewing for things like logic and control.

Unfortunately, R had a point. A. My suitcase is a disaster. The wheels are broken, and it isn't big enough for a get-away of this nature. B. He and I both know that lugging crap around an airport is among my least favorite things to do. Airports and I have a tentative relationship as is. And C. There will be plenty of room for both our things in one, large suitcase. The most logical thing to do would be pack together. We are going to the same place. We are a couple. What's the big deal?

In a phrase: freak flag exposure.

See, it is the goal of anyone in any relationship to minimize exposure of the other party to their various freak flags. This is not to say that secrets should be kept or lies told, it's just that no good can come from your boyfriend knowing you have 67 pair of shoes. If you have an addiction to shoe shopping that is crippling your financial future, fess up. If you have three pair of brown boots in various styles because that is what the life of an aspiring writer living in West Hollywood requires, rotate with frequency so he won't notice them all and get on with your totally stable life.

Packing is among my freak flags. Well, it's really wardrobe prep for event-based activities, but when those activities take place a flight away it manifests as packing. Yes, this makes me shallow and silly and far too over-analytical about what certain outfits say about my person. No, it's not changing.

R was not asking me to place our collective things in a properly sized case so that we might travel with greater ease. He was asking me to reveal that, *yes*, I am packing three dresses and one skirt/top combo for the rehearsal dinner because I'm not sure how fancy it is, when this damn self-tanner will finally kick in, and if formal jumpsuits are happening on the East Coast.

"This will be easy! Look! I'll pack right now and show you how much room you'll have," R said as he took 2.5 minutes to throw one pair of shoes, four shirts and some brown pants into the bag while keeping his focus squarely on a basketball game (*show off!*).

Oh, space is not my issue, I told him. All of those necessary items listed above will be fold-rolled to fit perfectly inside one half of a medium-sized suitcase. The issue, I thought to myself, is that my brain does that little rehearsal dinner dress routine you just read, and if I were R and I found that out, I'd be wondering what else a brain like that is capable of doing.

I pride myself on being a low to mid-range maintenance woman - fussy enough to take proper care of myself but not too fussy to drive an out-the-door-in-ten-minutes-man crazy. In *my* mind the fact that I must pack a hairdryer, diffuser attachment, straightener and curling iron keeps me squarely at the mid-range level. But what will R think when he finds a portable Sally Hansen Beauty supply store up against his one, half-filled dop kit?

In the end I swallowed my shame and let my freak flag fly. I may or may not have double-rolled two skirts inside another skirt sos to take my visual number of shirts packed from four to two, but there was no hiding the four pair of shoes: "Yes, two black pairs because if I end up going with the jump suit then it requires an espadrille, not a t-strap pump because t-strap pumps and formal jumpsuits aren't happening on either coast."

I'm pretty sure he thinks I'm crazy, but it appears he's letting this specific feature of my craziness fly un-criticized. I've decided this is either because he likes me regardless of what my brain does when packing or because he has an equally offensive freak flag factor up his sleeve that I'm dangerously close to exposing....

Ed Note: That was the first and last time we packed for a trip in one large suitcase. Instead R got me a new carry-on for my birthday that year. He said it was because I needed a new one, not because of the degree to which I freaked out about the whole joint packing charade, but I know he's lying.

The Annual Birthday Blog Post: Year 28

from 8/7/11

Do you only technically turn a year older at midnight in the time zone where you where born? So, if you're born in London but live in New York should you officially celebrate your birthday at 7:00PM the day before your date of birth?

This question only occurred to me today. Today, for the first time in my now 28 years, I opened my eyes in the same time zone where I opened those eyes for the very first time. It's possible that this is the most official birthday I've had since that very first one, which adds another milestone to the long list I've racked up since this same day last year.

Every year on my birthday I go back through this blog's archive and re-read the August 7th posts I've written prior. It's a bizarre trip down my public memory lane. Each time I go in thinking I'll read what that ridiculous 25-year-old wrote and laugh at how clueless she was, but I always come to the somewhat calming realization that I write the same thing every time:

At 25: *25, though, still holds a certain weight in my head – like this marker of actual adulthood signifying the end of getting away with blatant immaturity (in public). I feel like at 25 I have to sit myself down and say, "Okay, where are we? Oats, sewn; money, squandered; gateway drugs, tried; slippery slope through gateway, avoided; and metaphoric notches in (twin) bedposts, carved. Good work, now stop blacking out and start saving money." It's like from here on out I don't have to move forward in one, focused direction, but I can't blatantly move backward. I've made some solid ground and lived a life of which 80% could be shared with my parents; now my life's purpose is to not fuck it up.*

25, the year I do as I say and not as I want.

At 26: *We are the sum of our choices – trite but true - from as early on as we understand the concept of choice. But I think we sometimes forget that in choosing one thing, we're also choosing not another. This isn't an argument against having "it all" (there's no argument, you can't, but that's for another day). This is just a newly 26-year-old woman (who still feels like she should be referred to as "girl") realizing what she loves about her life but what she could and might soon leave behind now that with each passing year the future changes focus.*

At 27: *I actually want to have that pressure of feeling like there are items to check off in my 20s. I'm excited about drawing lines in the sand and pacing to meet them. The whole idea of the gravity of this point in life is exhilarating. It's not my scary age because I suspect I'll find my first grey hair before I turn 2-8. It was never about that. It's about the fact that the number 2-7- and where it falls in the scheme of life charges me with a motivation to commit to my passions and dive at the risks that requires.*

(God I'm a drama queen…)

And now at 28:

I've been thinking a lot about who I am versus where I am and where I've been - circumstance versus self, if you will.

This week, as if in preparation for this very post-writing purge, I had a mini break down about the degree to which my circumstances (long, exhausting hours at a job in my marketing career) are preventing me from reaching my true goals (a fully sustainable career as a writer). I moved 3,000 miles from my family to pursue those goals. I moved away from my very best friends to make them a reality. I sacrifice social life and personal time to write when I'm not at work. My circumstances affect me every day.

But I think part of being a mature person with their eyes squarely set on the prize has to do with not letting your circumstances bleed into your self. My circumstances are frustrating; my self remains hopeful. My circumstances have taken me very far from home; my self remains a fast-paced New Yorker with her family and friends on speed-dial. My circumstances make diving into a social life in L.A. harder because my time is so crunched; my self knows when to close the laptop and go to Wednesday night trivia with the gang.

When I look back at what I aimed to accomplish from 2-7 to 2-8, I see reason to be frustrated. I wanted to write more, produce more, network more, but what I all-too-often forget is that progress in your circumstance is one thing - your title, your salary, your number of books published. Progress in your self is something very different.

I moved clear across the country. I started a new job. I learned the ins and outs of the industry I've always aspired to join. I now know what steps I need and want to take for at least the next few years. Plus I met the guy with whom I've had the most meaningful relationship of my life.

As I read back on that list it looks far more significant than selling a script or staging a play. Either way, I'm happy, grateful, and lucky at 28 years old.

Today I will have a gigantic, Mexican brunch with my L.A. family and a romantic, seafood dinner with R. Tomorrow I will re-read this post, laugh at how deep I get after one bloody mary, and start freaking out about the fact that 30 is only two blog posts away...

Ed Note: I have a love hate relationship with this birthday blog posts. On the one hand, it's incredible to go back and visit myself turning another year older. On the other hand, they're always so annoyingly positive! Maybe that's because I tend to re-read them on days that are not my actual day of birth – days when I allow myself a more cynical perspective because I'm focused on the here-and-now not the greater picture.

It's like that age-old question, are drunk thoughts true thoughts? Are you more honest with yourself with the inebriated or is that just some hyper version of yourself talking...slash texting? Am I more honest with myself on these birthdays...or just more drunk?

I'm not sure we have a large enough sample size to tell. Maybe I'll keep writing these, blog or no blog, for the rest of my birthday-celebrating life (so, my life). Then I'll either have it figured out or not care to figure it out because I've already lived it.

Relationship Advice From Yet Another Dentist

from 10/24/11

Three years ago I went to the dentist in NYC and got completely unsolicited relationship advice.

Last week it happened again. Different city. Different dentist. Same barrage of advice on dating, relationships, marriage and children that I by no means requested. This time Dr. West Coast peppered in some general thoughts on both pop culture, history and philosophy.

Sos not to deny this bizarre occurrence its very own post, here goes.

LIFE ADVICE FROM DENTISTS (of mine): PART DEUX

- "Do not marry a man who is younger than 31-32...maybe 30 if he seems like he's got his noggin' on straight and his zipper zipped up."

- "If the guy you're with hasn't succeeded in his business by the time he's 30, he never will. I'm telling you. It's a fact."

- "People who get married in their early 20's have a real, real hard time making it. They just do. Plain and simple."

- "You wanna be real careful about being with a guy who makes less money than you, as a woman of course. If the man makes more money than the woman it becomes a giant mess. Equal pay, fine. Less, disaster. Really creates resentment, which - you know - *deeply* affects things in the bedroom."

- "You're probably going to want to convert to Judaism so your kids don't end up screwed up. I mean, I should say, do what you want religion-wise. I don't care if they're Buddhist, but make sure you present a unified front to the kids, religion-wise. They need that."

- "You know Thomas Jefferson was an atheist."

- "If you're gonna get re-married, make sure the guy isn't too close to his kids, if he has any from a previous marriage. That'll really screw things up."

- "I don't know much, but I'll tell you one thing I know for sure - that Marcus Bauchmann is gay as hell."

- "Whatta ya think - should I throw the dental gig away and get into that Dr. Phil work? Huh?"

And then he pinched my cheeks. The ones on my face, but still.

Those are the direct quotes I remember clear as day. There were also some comments on the dangers of fundamentalist Christians, how hard it is to believe in God after a tragedy and what happens if you have kids before you're married (note: nothing good).

Apparently somewhere inside my mouth there's a tattoo that reads, "Please provide me with tons of inappropriate and judgmental advice while you have my ability to respond in your hands, literally." That or I have the absolute worst taste in dentists...albeit consistent.

Ed Note: I had to stop seeing Dr. West Coast after he told me R was never going to propose because I already moved in. "Why would you give him the milk for free and then expect him to buy it??" I decided it wasn't worth the blog posts anymore. Also, he smelled like vodka.

This is Exactly What Happens When You Go For Your First Mammogram

from 1/24/12

I went for my very first mammogram recently because I'm getting close to 30, my insurance currently covers it, and sometimes my left boob is a little hurt-y. I realize that is TMI for many readers of this blog (hi Dad!), but I'm disclosing in the name of safety.

Because this was my very first mammogram, I was understandably nervous about the unknown details of the procedure. For how long, exactly, would I be naked? To what degree, exactly, would they be squeezing and shoving my boob into some freezing-cold device? Do I technically have enough boob to be squeezed and shoved into said device?

Here, to help you move more gracefully through your own first mammogram, is exactly what happened at mine:

1. I found a failed parking meter five minutes prior and two blocks away from my appointment! I took this as a sign from God that I did not have cancer.

2. My doctor's office - and perhaps yours? - now uses an iPad for new patients to enter in their medical history. Despite having an iPhone, it took me 15 minutes to complete my medical history on this device. It is worth noting that I do not technically have any medical history.

3. Ten or so minutes later, a Russian woman came to retrieve me. She called me Jessica, which made me feel older, more official and therefore like I had this mammogram thing totally under

control, even though that was in no way true.

4. The woman showed me to a dressing room and handed me a pink robe. She directed me to leave my bottoms on, make sure the robe opened to the front, and go sit in the pre-procedure waiting room when I was done. Then she left before I had time to ask her my 145 questions.

5. For the next eight to twelve minutes I hid in the mini room debating how, exactly, to tie the robe. Man oh man that robe! First of all, it was too long to be a tunic but too short to be a cute dress. Also, I had foolishly chosen to wear a knee-high boots that day, throwing off the already disastrous proportions. And finally, none of the placement of any of the eight ties closed the robe in any logical manner. I tied and re-tied that thing ten times before I was content enough to leave the little room, and even then there was a gaping hole around my chest area, of the not sexy-peep-hole variety.

Note: Upon arriving in the special waiting room I discovered that the reason why the robes look like crap is because they're actually the ones that are meant to tie in the *back* (some other rookie didn't follow directions). Brand new iPads for the office are a lot more affordable if you're stealing gowns from the hospital, aren't they...

6. Another ten or so minutes went by before another Russian woman came to get me for the procedure. Her name was Oksana, and she actually did look like what Oksana Baiul might look like 17 years and 35 pounds after the '94 Olympics. As such, I convinced myself that she was Oksana Baiul.

7. Oksana Baiul brought me to a room with curiously good lighting and instructed me to lie on my side. She then squirted a gel fluid onto my boob (which was blessedly warm) and preceded to rub my boob using one of those x-ray sticks they use to tell pregnant women if they're having a boy or a girl. I did not laugh even though it tickled like hell. I remain very proud of this fact.

Now *heeere's* where things got tricky.

Oksana Baiul lingered around several areas of the boob and took what I believe were photos based on a camera-like clicking sound. I had a clear view of the monitor showing the picture of whatever results from the x-ray wand, but I was too afraid to look, so I just focused on the ceiling the whole time and tried not to giggle.

After an amount of time that I felt was particularly long based on absolutely no prior experience with this process, the woman who stole Nancy Kerrigan's gold medal gave me a towel to wipe off the remaining goop. She then said two things in what I believed to be a very grave voice: "Do you have any family history of breast cancer?" (I do not) and "I need to go review your films with the doctor." And then she left, rather quickly in my opinion.

And so I'm like, *okay, I have obviously cancer.*

Long procedure? Family history question? Immediate need to review films with the doctor? I've watched six out of eight seasons of Grey's. I know imminent bad news when they're keeping it from you. This. Was. Bad.

I spent the next 15 minutes deciding how to tell my parents and outlining the book I would write once I *kicked this thing*! (It was obviously a collection of humorous essays). I may or may not have also practiced my reaction to the news, out loud. I was going to go with a combination of, "oh god..." and, "are you sure?"

While the above paragraph is written in a comedic tone, there was NOTHING comical about sitting in that room for ten minutes and waiting to find out that I did NOT, in fact, have cancer. As it turns out the doctor ALWAYS has to review the films and ALWAYS comes in to let you know the results.

Note to Mammography Offices: THAT'S a detail you want to share with your patients before the procedure begins. It's MISSION CRITICAL info folks.

After the doctor informed me that I did not have cancer based on the x-ray stick results, I asked her if Oksana Baiul was going to come back and get me for the actual mammogram part. After all *that* unexpected nonsense, I was itching to shove my boob in the freezing cold machine and get outta there!

That's when I found out that I was only scheduled for a sonogram, not a mammogram. Apparently those are the preferred method of screening these days.

Note: I did end up seeing the mammogram machine inside another examination room, and it didn't look that scary.

Ed Note: If you are over 25 and have not been for your first mammogram, ask your general practitioner whether or not they think you should go. If they say yes, ask whether or not it will be an actual mammogram or just the fake one I got, and continue to get every year. And remember, do NOT wear boots of any kind on the day of your procedure. A sneaker or flat will look best with the robe. Good luck to you.

How to Prepare to Move in With Your Boyfriend

from 3/15/12

There may come a time in your life when you and your boyfriend will decide you're ready to live together, and when that time comes, you may or may not have some serious prep work to do.

Here, in no particular order, are my personal recommendations:

1. Arrange an informal meeting in which you discuss the cosmetic improvements you'd each like to make to the apartment. I recommend this meeting take place while the TV is on or one/both of you have had a few cocktails.

2. At said meeting you want to be sure to get *all* those preferred cosmetic improvements out on the table to avoid conversations like the following:

    - R: I think I do want some extra drawers for clothes in the closet.
    - Me: Okay, great.
    - Me: ...is this a session where we each say the additional apartment things we've been thinking we want?
    - R: No.
    - Me: Right...

3. Use feeling words to explain your desires for the shared space. Things like, "I feel like a new plant would look nice here!" or, "I feel like we could save space if we organize these utensils!" or, "I feel like we should paint that wall neon yellow!...?"

4. Decide how many pair of shoes you can realistically part with on your own, remove those shoes from your closet without assistance, and bring those shoes to the donation center without

anyone checking the bag before it goes. If asked, report back that you donated, "a whole lot of shoes!"

5. When asked why the belts need their own drawer, don't say, "because the clutches and small purses have their own drawer, so why shouldn't the belts?" That's not constructive, or logical.

6. If then asked, "When was the last time you even wore some of these belts?" don't quote the actual dates you last wore some of those belts. That's just weird. Why would you even know that?....

7. Yes, purple is a wonderful, wonderful color that can, in some circumstances, be considered gender neutral. Still, it's best to get over your affinity for it before moving into an apartment with a man, who is straight.

8. Decide what items you need from IKEA by perusing their extensive online site, then elect one member of your party to actually go retrieve those items. This move alone will add 10+ years to your relationship.

9. Now would be the time to share specific lifestyle quirks that are just bound to rear their ugly heads. It's not *that* weird that you really want the loose end of the toilet paper to fall *behind* and not in front of the roll.

10. Similarly, you don't have to make up excuses for why you want certain things a certain way in your new shared space. You can just say you want your clothes to be on the left side of the closet instead of the right. You don't have to make up some weird story about how, because you're left handed, they should be on the left so you don't bump elbows with your boyfriend if you're both inside the closet selecting clothing side-by-side.

11. And, most importantly, when people ask how the move prep is going, don't make a face like you just ate fat-free, plain Greek yogurt for the first time, especially if your boyfriend is sitting

directly next to you.

You're confident in your relationship! You're excited about this next step! And, if you're anything like me, you're insanely grateful that this man has agreed to live with you, despite your obvious quirks...and not-so-obvious number of shoes.

Ed Note: R and I have survived 1+ years of life together in our small, one-bedroom apartment and I can say with confidence that we have never fought about elements in the shared space. One-time things got a little dicey after I suggested we make a standing garden out of a shipping palette at 5PM on a Sunday evening, but that technically happened on the patio, not inside the apartment.

To what do I attribute this happy life inside a small, IKEA-clad space: I have absolutely no idea. It could be "love" but it could also be the fact that we both like Man Men-era furniture and a clean kitchen counter. I'll get back to you in another 1+ years. Hopefully things will be just as blissful, and R will still have no idea where I'm hiding the other dozen pair of shoes...

My Secret Annual Birthday Routine

from 8/2/12

Today I will do what is, perhaps, the most ridiculous ceremonial thing out of all the ridiculous ceremonial things I do (treat myself to a fancy hotel dirty martini every time I finish a script being a close second on the list).

I will go to the Bank of America and take out $40 from the ATM. I will have the bank teller break that $40 into a twenty and two tens. I will put one twenty and one ten of those forty dollars into the front fold of my wallet. Then I will take that $30 to the Forever 21 at the 3rd Street Promenade where I will spend it, and not a penny more than it, on a dress to wear on my birthday - just as I have done every single year since I turned…wait for it…21. I warned you it was ridiculous.

This whole birthday dress routine did not start out as an annual event. I actually didn't even realize it was happening until roughly 24. That should prove to you just how often I'm in a Forever 21 buying a $29.99 dress.

It dawned on me somewhere around the empire waist white lace number (24th, Boat Basin Party, NYC). Before that there was a one shoulder black tank and navy green military-style Capri pant (21, Leggett's Bar and Grill, Manasquan, NJ) and something short, tight and red (22nd, Sway Club, NYC). This is before Facebook had photo capabilities (remember that??), so I can't be entirely sure. There have since been two floral maxi dresses, one with big, pastel flowers (25th, Tortilla Joe's, NYC), and one with tiny, earth tone flowers (28th, Malibu Wines, CA); a white, layered number with a cute racer back cut (26th, The Dove, NYC), and this pink, fringy situation somewhere in the mix (27th? no... 23rd? I'm missing a year...).

But once I realized I was ringing in each year of life in a one-wear frock from a place where middle school girls shop I thought, *awesome, I've got to see this one straight through to 29!*

Anndd, here we are at 29. Time flies when you're dressing like time isn't flying...

I like to think my annual shopping treat is like a mini microcosm of my progression in life from 21-30. At first I did not have enough money to shop at stores where they sell clothes made of real fabric. Then I had slightly more money, but I wanted to save it for things other than trendy party dresses. Now I have those things I saved for and a bit more money in the bank, but I'm totally conditioned to gawk at $100 price tags (or, apparently, $31.00 price tags). I like crazy, loud clothing, and my style changes from one year to the next. Ergo, the F21 is my Mecca.

I still have each and every one of my dirt-cheap birthday dresses rudely taking up space in the closet R and I now share. They're supposed to self-destruct after one wear, but they keep on keeping on, like little hanging metaphors of 20-something life.

This year I'm focused on a tea length mustard yellow skirt and sheer, white printed tank, and I know I'll find it because there is nothing the Forever 21 doesn't carry - *nothing*.

As for next year - we'll see. Maybe I'll up the ante to $40 and change the venue to Nordstrom Rack. Or maybe I'll just keep buying a $30 dress at a store intended for kids for the rest of my birthday celebrating life...

Ed Note: I am now just one month away from my 30th birthday, *and while I have no idea how I'll react to the momentous ending of my 20-something life, I know I'll be doing it in a chic, $29.99 ensemble from Forever21. If they 'aint broke after one wear, why shop elsewhere?*

Yes, that's my personal slogan for F21. I thought about contacting the company to offer it up as a genius new ad campaign in exchange for a lifetime supply of clothing, but at $29.99 I should probably just pay for the damn dresses like an actual adult.

Today Is My 29th Birthday And I Feel...

from 8/7/12

...nothing in particular.

I've been dreading this post - the one I've written every August 7th for the past five years - because I felt I hadn't come to any conclusions about my own 2-9 mark. I didn't feel particularly anxious or particularly calm. I didn't have very many regrets about my 20s, and I know that those I do have are just a product of peer slash self pressure (I don't have a three picture deal!! I haven't written a successful young adult book series!!!).

I'm healthier than I've ever been thanks to more regular flossing and less regular dirty martini drinking. This weird area on my hip hurts when I go on the elliptical for longer than 30 minutes, but I'm going to chalk that up to the fact that 29 is not 18 and be grateful I only have three strands of grey hair (used to...plucked those puppies the minute I found them). I am in a relationship with the absolute right person, and he makes every aspect of my life better every day. And even though they're 3K miles away, my loving and supportive family remains loving and supportive in a way that feels like they're right here in L.A. So is life a blissful place of self-acceptance and wise perspective on love and life? Absolutely not.

Every other day I wonder if I'm making the right decision about how I balance my work and my passions (note: I'm not, and I'm working on that.). Sometime around 3pm every single day I almost fall asleep and think to myself, *oh my god am I tired because I'm old?? I am!! I'm tired because I'm old!!* I cannot just eat a bagel and cream cheese every morning for breakfast; my blood is Italian and Jewish, and my thighs are now following suit. There are days when I wonder if I'm waiting too long to start a family, and I'm not even married or engaged yet. When I'm sitting in bumper to bumper traffic on Olympic at 5PM I think, all of my family and most of my closest friends are across the entire country; *what am I doing here?!* And I now have the potential to get a hangover after two drinks. TWO DRINKS PEOPLE!

This list of life pluses and minuses is only meant to prove that "29" isn't any one thing, much like 25,6,7 and 8. I have pride, and I have disappointments. I feel young, and I feel old. I am comfortable in my skin, and I am still totally self-conscious at times. I both know what I want to come in my life and have no idea how or when it will happen. Sometimes that is totally and completely overwhelming and sometimes that is somehow entirely manageable.

But I think at 29, versus 25,6,7, or 8, I realize that it's not about knowing everything, it's about handling the inability to truly know *anything*. Any life worth living is a balancing act of passions and obligations, family and friends, fears and desires. I have not fully mastered any of those things, but on any given day I can feel in control of one or some. Those moments on those days feels good, and that good feeling gives me hope, and that hope makes me excited about all the next days to come.

So after four years of writing 800 word essays on what it means to turn another year older inside this all-powerful 20 to 30-year-old range, I don't have a thesis statement on the final 20-something number. Today I feel great. Tomorrow I may feel tired or frustrated or fat. By Thursday, who knows? Life isn't measured by what we think we know but rather by how we know to live. And at 29 I'm proud to say that I feel like I've finally got a handle on how to be alive.

Ed Note: Still kicking and generally just as sure of how to do it. In other words, I have no idea how to reflect on this because I still have no idea how I feel about turning 30...

Why I Haven't Written Lately and What it's Made Me Realize

from 8/21/12

I haven't written a blog post in over a week and a half, and I'm mad about it. I'm mad, and I'm disappointed, and I'm stressed.

I'm mad because I made a personal commitment to writing twice a week, and I haven't followed through lately. I'm disappointed because I know that as a writer you're nothing without your audience, and you lose that audience the minute you become unreliable. And I'm stressed because this isn't the only writing that I haven't had time to do. There is a script that needs revision and another that needs to be started, and there are people waiting for both.

- "I think I'm going through a really hard time," I told R last night.
- "I think so too," he said, "what are we doing to do about it?"
- "I don't know," I said.
- "That's not true," he said.

The first issue I always raise when the topic of making writing my full-time life presents is the cost of health insurance in this country. "Do you know the cost of individual health insurance in this country??" I bark at R when he tells me to take the leap away from my full time job. "It's astronomical! Plus I have a car, and car insurance, and student loans, and rent and general life needs. I mean I could probably eek by freelancing...if it wasn't for the cost of health insurance. It's really outrageous."

After I'm forced to admit that there are dozens of ways to make roughly 1K per month (my car is cheap, and I now live in a small apartment with R), I turn to the issue of "deserving it." That's the only way I can explain feeling like I have no "right" - at this age, in this economy, given the numbers stacked against writers - to say, "who cares! I want to do it! Be damned, world!"

I think this particular neurosis stems from the fact that I've only ever viewed writing as a passion that very lucky people get to do after the entire universe has confirmed that they're allowed to do it.

> "How exactly does the universe confirm that you're allowed to be a writer?" R asked. "I'm not sure," I say, "but I'll know it when it's confirmed."

People are struggling just to get by, I say. My parents didn't spend their life savings on my education so I could quit a job, I say. People will think I'm just another starry-eyed writer in Los Angeles, I say.

- "Who cares?" R says.
- "I care!" I say.
- "Why do you care so much?" R says.
- "I don't know!" I say, "I'm still working on that!"

From there come the list of my "I'll do it when" terms, which include but are not limited to:

- "Okay, I'll do it when this most recent script is finished."
- "Okay, I'll do it after this most recent script is finished *and* I have a really good indication that it's going to lead to something."
- "Okay, I'll do it when I'm certain I've stacked up enough freelance work to pay the bills."
- "Okay, I'll do it when I've saved exactly six months worth of living expenses. You know, they say that's exactly how much you should have to consider going freelance."
- "Okay, I'll do it when I've saved exactly nine months worth of living expenses. They say six months is all you really

need, but I'll just go ahead and make it nine to be extra safe."

Except at this point the script is finished, there's a good indication it's going to lead to something, and I have 8.5 months of expenses saved. Regarding the, "stacking up of freelance work," I have some leads, but it's hard to focus on them when you're working the kind of hours I have been this past year.

"What are you really so afraid of?" R asks.

This was last night. It was also the third time in the past six weeks that he's asked me that question, and I've responded with tears. "No, no, no. Don't cry!" he says, "This should be the most exciting time in your life! You're finally on the cusp of doing what you've planned to do for *years*. Why do you keep crying about it?"

In my head I start in on the health insurance issue, then the general finance fears, then the "who am I do just up and be a writer?" hang up and then, "I'll do it when x, y, z details make it wholly clear that this is a 100% safe thing to do." Yes, all of those are legitimate factors, in one way or another, but they're not the real issue.

The real issue is that I'm afraid I'll fail. I'm afraid I'm not good enough to make it. I'm afraid I don't know how to be a full-time writer. I'm afraid that my self worth will plummet, and I'll develop crippling writer's block, and I'll end up producing less product that I even do now.

...And then I won't have full-time work, and everyone will think I'm a fool, and I'll go into debt, and I'll have to move back into my parents basement, and I won't be able to afford health insurance. It's really *very* expensive, you know.

- "Do you really think you're going to fail?" R says.
- "No," I say, "Not *that* badly, at least."

And then I say the thing that I always say once the conversation reaches this point: If I'm really honest with myself, I'm more afraid that I'm never going to do it.

A college professor once told me that when you find yourself at a crossroads of confidence, it's often most helpful to simply say the truths. Don't get caught up in the "what ifs" and "maybes" and "I don't knows." Say the things you absolutely know, and see what path they suggest. So, here goes:

- Nothing has ever made me feel as fulfilled, excited, engaged or proud as my writing.
- Over the past five years I have developed a loyal audience through this blog. You continue to read my writing, tell me you enjoy it, and often ask for more.
- I have been paid to write by many publications.
- People within the creative community here in L.A. have expressed interest and confidence in my ability to have a writing career.
- I have previous experience as a waitress, babysitter, retail associate, tutor, and PA.
- I will not go hungry. I will not have to move back into my parents' basement. And I will very likely never go without health insurance.
- Also, I have never had writer's block.

This is a turning point in my life and in my writing, but when I look at those truths, it's a turn I've already made. I am a writer. I have been a writer for years. The only difference between the writer I currently am and the writer I intend to be very soon is the time I commit to writing. Being a writer is not about how much money you make writing, no matter how much I need that validation to call myself a success. There will come a time when I make nothing, and that's something I have to get used to. There will also hopefully come a time when I make lots, but that isn't something I can bank on. Now it's time to take a leap of faith rooted in a list of truths and backed by the support of lots of people, including all of you.

"And the day came when the risk to remain tight in a bud was more painful than the risk it took to blossom," Anaïs Nin said.

I think I'm arriving at that day, and I think I know what I need to do. No. Sorry. I am arriving at that day, and I know what I need to do.

I guess when you think about it, the cost of monthly health insurance is pretty cheap when you weigh it against the cost of never doing the one thing you aspire to do in life.

Ed Note: If there's a theme to this entire blog, it's got to be that damn Anaïs Nin quote that I've used not one but three times over the course of the posts in this book.

A few days after I wrote this post, I told my boss that I needed to move on from my job. Three months after that, I left full-time work, hopefully for good. Two months after becoming unemployed, I picked up a freelance writing job that included health insurance. I now write for that employer – E!'s Fashion Police – five days per week until approximately 1PM and focus on my personal writing – scripts of all kinds – for the afternoon. I'm still afraid I'm going to fail. Every once in awhile I kiss my health insurance card for good luck. But bottom line, I'm doing it. And it's so much more awesome than it is scary.

Dating Advice for Baby Zadie

from 10/23/12

One of my very best friends just gave birth to the very first baby among my set of very best friends. Her name is Zadie Patricia, and she is perfect. I know people say that about all babies, but they're wrong. This baby is the most perfect baby of them all, and that's a fact.

After Zadie was born I got to thinking about dating advice for babies. Not, as in, how they should go about dating other babies. That is a hysterical, but mostly gross thought. I mean, if I could whisper little pieces of advice into baby Zadie's ears now to prevent her from heartbreak and wasted time later, what would I say?

They say dating habits are learned very early on, and that the confidence to date the right people is something you start developing at birth, so why not "Einstein baby" in a little practical advice to prevent some tear-stained diary pages later on?

Here is what I have for baby Zadie so far:

- If it's between the class "bad boy" and the class "clown" you go clown every time. The reasons the bad boy is bad are way deeper/worse/dark & twisty than the reasons the clown is funny - for now at least.

- Nine times out of 10, a guy's favorite "outfit" of yours will be your jeans and flannel combo, so don't stress too much about looking perfect.

- If you say, "no," and he says, "come on...don't be a prude..." you run for the hills.

- If you say, "no," and he says, "you have to...I'll have the worst blue balls if you don't..." you tell him that your wise, old Auntie Jessie told you blue balls are a crock of shit, and then you run for the hills.

- Ariel = Bad Disney Princess, Belle = Better Disney Princess, Jasmine = Best Disney Princess.

- I don't know if people will still be making phone calls when you are of dating age, but if they still are, make sure a guy does it more than once at the onset of your relationship. It means he is brave, and you should only be dating the bravest of men.

- Chances are you won't look back on life and says, "gosh I really should have lost my virginity sooner!" Keep that in mind on Prom night.

- The number of best girlfriends you have should always be greater than or equal to the number of boyfriends you've had in the past year. I can't explain why this is so, but it is.

- You should either *always* trust your judgment after a few cocktails or *never* trust your judgment after a few cocktails. You'll know which after the first time you call/text/kiss a guy after a few cocktails.

- It is way sadder to be lonely inside a relationship than to be lonely *for* a relationship. Try not to learn by experience on this one.

And - most importantly - don't date anyone who isn't as kind, loving, romantic, smart, brave, caring, funny, and sincere as your Dad. Not that you'll have any trouble snagging exactly that kind of man since you are the daughter of your absolutely incredible Mom.

Ed Note: Several months ago Baby Zadie met her first potential boyfriend, Harrison. I'm told she wore a simple sundress (total guy magnet), started coy but warmed up quickly (she may or may not have just woken up…), and left him in a total state of wonder (which, at two months old is pretty much his MO about the world, but still). I think we're off to a very strong start.

Today Is The Last Day Of My Current Life

from 1/11/12

...dramatic, but true. As of tomorrow, I am officially/finally/hopefully forever, a full time writer.

GOD it feels good to type that.

For the past two years I have worked nine to five, six, and sometimes ten as the Director of Branded Entertainment at a LA-based production company. Before that I was a branded content producer at a NYC-based media agency, and right after college I worked in PR for a wedding website and as a sponsorship account manager at the Tribeca Film Festival. That's seven years of jobs that were fulfilling and interesting, but not my ultimate passion. I did them to earn money and gain experience in the entertainment industry while chugging toward my writing career.

Today, thanks to a combination of the money I've saved, the progress I've made with my writing and the courage I've somehow harnessed, I'm leaving that behind to start an entirely new chapter. In a way, it's just a full-fledged version of a chapter I started a very long time ago, with this little blog.

My goal is and has always been to write for a living. I now believe I will achieve that goal. Those seem like two simple sentences, but they are probably that most difficult conclusions I've ever made.

I have a million and one thoughts about this decision and what's to come as a result, but I'll explore those here over the coming weeks (with ALL the new time I'll have on my hands!). For now I just want to say THANK YOU.

Starting this blog gave me a reason to write every day. Writing everyday defined my voice as that writer. Sharing that specific voice online resulted in friends encouraging me to write plays, television and film samples. Experiencing those forms of writing made me realize my passion for that specific writing medium. My passion for that medium inspired me to move to Los Angeles where more friends shared my new writing with their industry contacts. Two of those contacts were literary managers who now represent me as a television and film writer. It's crazy to trace it back just that simply, but those are the steps, and you can make them happen too.

I'm not sure exactly what's around the bend. I have some projects in play, I have some ideas on the horizon, and I have back-up freelance work if none of those pan out.

But as of tomorrow I am a writer - first, foremost, and (hopefully) forever.

Ed Note: At the publishing of this book it will be nine months since I left full-time work. Since then I have not turned back. It just felt way too good to type "writer" under the occupation field for my taxes, so I think I'll just have to find a way to type that in for the rest of my life.

10 Things Every 30-year-old Should Be Prepared To Say
from 3/13/12

Guys, it pains me to say this, but we're not kids anymore. I'm told that happened around 18, but nicer people claim 21. As far as I'm concerned it still hasn't happened, but I am currently staring down the barrel of a gun called 30, so the gig might in fact be up.

And so in an effort to prepare ourselves for life as the adults we've apparently been for several years at this point, I've compiled a list of key "phrases" that we should all possess the chutzpah to say. They may not be things you have said or things you'll ever need to say, but if the moment arises, I feel that you best be prepared to say them:

10. Listen, I need you to buy me tampons at the grocery store. Just grab the first multi-pack you see and get the hell out of there.

9. Bottom line: we can't make any new friends until after the wedding invites go out.

8. I'm sorry, did you just say you got pregnant on the VERY FIRST TIME TRYING?!

7. The rules of this wedding dress shopping session are simple. If I love it, you love it.

6. I don't want to have sex tonight, and I don't have a reason.

5. Right, but can you describe to me exactly how it will feel approximately 30 seconds *before* my water breaks?

4. Thank you for this offer. Given my experience level and past performances, I'd like to see if your company can come up 10K on the base starting salary.

3. Of course I'd love a little girl, but I'll just be happy if the baby is healthy.

2. You don't have to go through with this wedding, sweetie. We'll get you out of here and handle telling everyone.

1. Oh my god...my mother used to say that exact same thing...I'm becoming my mother...

Ed note: I'd like to add the following to the list in light of lessons learned between the first publication of this post.

- *I appreciate the suggestion, but it's not your wedding.*

- *Doctor, is there some kind of test I can take to determine exactly when I'm going to start having trouble getting pregnant?*

- *It's not me, it's you.*

Why I Knew the Answer to "Will You Marry Me" was "YES"

from 4/30/13

Believe it or not, I'm not a hopeless romantic. Not deep down at least.

Despite my public love of all-things Nora Ephron and private love of way too many things Nicholas Sparks, I don't believe in love at first sight, I'm not so sure about soul mates, and three years ago, I couldn't have even told you what I was looking for in a future husband. I'm not quite a cynic, but I'm definitely a realist when it comes to matters of love.

But over the past three years, I came to realize that all that realism was just fear. Love is scary, commitment is scarier, and marriage is a step beyond all of that. You have to give more of yourself than you ever realized you had to give while taking on more of another person than you could have fathomed existed. You have to have a certain level of immeasurable passion in your heart and an equal amount of impossible to weigh knowledge in your head. And you have to trust fully and completely without ever having all the evidence you'll need answer the almighty-est of questions: will I love this person forever? Will he love me? Will we make it 'til death do us part?

People always say, "when you know, you know," but I never believed them. The realist in me thought, what does that even mean? What do you "know" when you "know?" How does a person get to the point where they are sure enough to make the most life changing of life-changing decisions?

I don't know, but I did it on Saturday afternoon in a private nook on New York City's High Line Park (because that was the site of our first east coast date). I don't remember a word I said beyond YES. I don't have a clue what R said beyond "marry me?" but in the three minutes before he asked (when I finally realized something might be up) and the endless hours that followed (when *all* of our family and so many of our friends showed up for the post-engagement celebration) I was sure. I've been sure about saying "yes" for a very long time. And the only words I can use to describe that feeling of complete and utter certainty are, "you know when you know."

But that bothered me last night on the flight back to L.A. as I thought over this big deal of a blog post while staring at my brand new, amazingly sparkly, absolutely-perfect-in-every-way-ring (like !!!!!!!). I'm an overly verbose, over-thinker who has been over-sharing about relationship issues for years. How can I just leave it at the cliché that left me feeling ill equipped for all these years? And, more importantly, how can I - the self-proclaimed "rational romantic" - have an answer without a rationale?

And so, I feel like I owe it to myself and all of you to end this ridiculous charade around certainty, to explain even a few of those inexplicable feeling you should have before you're ready to say yes, and, because he deserves it so, *so* much, to explain why I specifically said yes to R.

Here goes - in all it's mushy, over-the-top, I've-been-engaged-for-48-hours glory. You were warned.

- I *feel* the love I have for R - like feel it in my bones and sometimes my belly but most often that area where I also feel heartburn after too much good food. I look at him sometimes - like after he does something particularly perfect or particularly imperfect - and actually *feel* love.

- I see R feel that same love for me. It looks like total adoration mixed with general amazement, a little bit of passion and total satisfaction. The result is something really awkward and goofy, but pretty obvious.

- I respect R like a mentor or family member or really impressive celebrity who I look at and think - *damn*, that person is just killing it at life. I aspire to be more like them. I think, "I'd hire R to do anything," and, "God, R is good at what he does," and, "If anyone can do it, R can."

- I'm able to envision the hard times that will absolutely come and see myself handling them with R. I can see how it plays out, even the scary stuff. It's a bit dark to picture tragedy, but there's such solace in knowing how he will love me through that - how he will be there for me. It makes the scary things less scary.

- I don't "need" R in the fish-needs-water sense or "want" R in the girl-needs-shoes sense, but I *want* to *need* him. This is tricky, but I think of it as having the desire to let go of the control in my life so that there is room to let R help me live more fully, safely, happily, you name it. It also lets R love me like he needs to, in addition to loving me like I need to be loved. Full disclosure (though we're *way* beyond that...) this was the hardest part for me.

- I notice that R is the same man in every element of his life, and that integrity of self has flowed over into our relationship. We are the same couple no matter to venue or audience, and because of that people *know* us - as individuals but also as a couple. And it feels really good to be known by other people.

- Life is more fun, exciting, full, challenging and just freaking awesome every single day because of R. Point blank. No further explanation.

These are solid reasons that I can explain and exhibit. They're tangible. You can see them for yourself. But when R sat me down on the bench just away from the crowds for his pre-proposal, speech he told me the story he tells me every year on the anniversary of the day we met (which, yes of course, was three years ago this past Saturday - the day he proposed). He told me that when I walked into the bar he saw me from across the room and knew I was the girl he was going to marry. And I cried like I cry every single year when he tells me because, despite all of the logic in my head that says that kind of thing is impossible, I believe him.

I believe him because on our first "official" date - a few days after we met - I stared into his eyes as he talked about his love of music, and his relationship with his nephews, and his family's house on Copake Lake, and I knew too.

Because when you know, you know.

My wish for every single one of you is that you feel the same inexplicable, heart-bursting feeling that comes from saying YES when the question is finally asked. It is pure magic.

Ed Note: This is both the hardest post I've ever had to write and also the easiest one I've ever written. It was hard because I wanted it to be perfect, but it was easy because once I started writing, I couldn't and didn't stop. Seems appropriate, right?

How Registering For Wedding Gifts Is Nothing Like Shopping For Shoes

from 5/14/13

Registering was one of the things I was most looking forward to about being engaged. I think it's one of the things everyone is most looking forward to about being engaged. How could you not be excited about a 100X-the-gifts-Christmas in which you pick every single item...using a super neat-o electronic gun?

Add to that the fact that shopping is among the things I do best in life - wrapped baked brie in the shape of things, give dating advice I'm unqualified to give, write the dialogue of sassy gay men and shop - but shopping is top among that impressive list of very necessary life skills.

Registering is just shopping on a more awesome, exciting, life-changing scale, I thought. You're not searching for an outfit to wear to some lame event; you're on a mission to discover a dish pattern that you and your future *husband* will use to eat all the meals of your life! This isn't some quick trip to the Payless to pick up Christian Siriano's latest dirt-cheap design; this is a daylong venture to select the items that will make your future house a home!

I was going to *kill* it at registering. I was going to be as swift and decisive as I was thoughtful and team oriented. I was going to make sure R's desires for the stuff of our life were as equally represented as mine. I was going to shoot that red laser at the bar code and hit it on the first time, *every time!*

Except for one little issue...

I suck at registering.

Not, like, I couldn't get the red laser beam to hit the right part of the very tiny black bar code (though I couldn't do that either. *literally* not once). I mean I am very bad at the entire act of selecting items that will serve as wedding gifts. So bad, in fact, that I have handed over the task of registry selection and management to R. I'm taking on more of a consulting role. It's the most I can handle, and it's touch-and-go at that.

This shocking turn of events all started at the Crate&Barrel on Beverly Drive around 3pm Saturday afternoon. I was all dressed up in my registering outfit (pleated salmon skirt and pale blue striped button-down, tied at the waist), and rearing to go. We had just completed the research portion of our trip and were now firmly and jointly decided on C&B as destination number one.

"Can I help you?" the nice-looking blonde lady asked me as I bounded toward her with a look that I intended to say, "we're here to REGISTER!!!" but probably said, "Look out! I'm about to hug you so hard!!!"

Disappointment #1 - there is no "congrats, you're registering!" gift, which I really still can't believe. I mean, we're committing to advertise the look and feel of the products in your store for the rest of our lives, and you don't have a glass of chilled champagne on the ready?

Disappointment #2 - they walk you over to an in-store kiosk and let you do it yourself. It's a 15 second process, and they don't even wait around to watch you do it. At first I thought that's because they were going to get the champagne, but you know how that turned out.

Now I am certain of very few things in life, but my sense of style is something I've known since the day I was old enough to dress myself (read: one and a half). Yes, that style has exhibited mostly in the form of clothing, shoes and accessories, but what is kitchenware if not the accessories of the kitchen? Yes, these items would serve a function, but selecting them would be like creating one giant outfit...that R and I would collectively wear...for the rest of our lives together...

That very deep, very overwhelming realization occurred to me just as we approached the large pasta bowls section of the store.

    "Okay, so something durable and white, right?" R said as he practiced scanning bar codes and nailing it on the first time *every single time*.
    "Um...I....well....yes?" I said."
"I like this one. Do you like this one?" R said.
    "Um...I...well...yes?" I said, as I backed slowly away from the bowl.
    "Good. Do you want to scan the first thing?"
"No...I...well...no," I said, as I turned in the other direction and froze in place staring directly at the giant glass jugs for water section (because they have one of those).
    "Are you freezing up?" R said.

Freezing up is something I do when faced with a decision that I am not prepared to make, generally one involving money. For example I frequently freeze up when R wants to book super expensive airlines tickets four months in advance of a flight. I'd rather just hold out and hope there are super cheap airlines tickets, say, three days before we need to fly.

    "I am," I said. "I am freezing up...So many decisions to make...and things are so expensive...and what if we don't like the plates in a few years...and should everything be stainless steal or ceramic white...or *both*?!"

Two hours later we walked out of the Crate&Barrel with a six-page print out of the items that will define our life, though I'm supposed to stop calling them that.

I survived the experience but I would not say I quite "killed it." I would say it came close to killing me, but that would be over dramatic, and I swore I wouldn't be one of those over dramatic brides...publicly.

Turns out my training in quantity versus quality purchasing over the years does not make me an expert in the art of registering. I'm more an expert in the art of buying a $20 birthday dress from Forever21 on sale for $14.99. Then when that dress falls apart six months later I buy another one in a totally different style because by that point neon is in and empire waists are out. They don't make La Creuset in neon, which is good because I'm already having a hard enough time deciding if I want the red or the yellow (yellow, right?). I think I'll end up letting R decide. Turns out he's *amazing* at registering. Which I guess makes sense given the fact that he spends legitimate money on legitimate clothing items once every few years. I now know that he's been secretly training to register for wedding gifts with that move...

So, fine. R can have this round. I am happily settled in my consulting role (which sort of goes, "okay let's register for that then I'll think about it for the next several months, change it twice and ultimately return it for something else). But if it turns out he's better at making DIY centerpieces than I am, I'm calling this whole thing off.

Ed Note: I am pleased to say that while registering is nothing like shopping for shoes, receiving gifts off your registry is just like opening shoes you ordered online. That's a silver lining I can get behind.

Dating Rules From My Future Self

from 6/8/13

I spent most of Thursday afternoon reading through the first two years of these blog posts, partly because I've been feeling nostalgic (already) but mostly because I'm prepping a little surprise (it's this book!).

I learned several things about my former self through all that reading - I had absolutely no idea what I wanted to do with my life; I spent an inordinate amount of time at bars; I had exactly the same amount of shoes - but paramount among the themes was this idea of "the rules."

I wrote a whole post about how to initiate communication with a potential date via Facebook. 500 words. I'd link to it here, but I'm too ashamed of the fact that it exists. There was a post on the proper way to speak to an attractive person at a bar. There was a whole expose about whether or not one should hook up on the second date. I did a *full week* on what constitutes cheating.

I was obsessed with this idea of modern dating etiquette, or, more specifically, how to survive dating unscathed. I was all about removing any grey area so that time wasn't wasted and feelings weren't hurt. I really, truly thought that there should be an agreed-upon way we should all be going about this insane "process" - from how to text your true intentions to when to sleep with someone to ensure they won't start dating you just for the sex.

If there are hard and fast rules - my former self seemed to think - then we can know with certainty whether someone is really interested or just using us. And if we know that, then we can avoid wasting time on a relationship that's ultimately going to hurt us more than it will help us.

"It's like gambling," I told R this morning as we walked to Ed's Diner on Robertson (the *best* eggs in Los Angeles). "In blackjack there's that whole 'what the house would say' rule that usually prevents you from busting. That's how I used to look at dating and relationships. What move is offer the least risk and most potential reward."

R liked that, but mostly because he taught me everything I know about gambling even though, as he reminded me this morning, I tried to hit on a 21 in Vegas...more than once.

"I get that," he said, "I think we were all doing that in our early 20s. But why do you think we were grasping at rules so much?"

I'm still not sure I know the answer to that question. Part of me thinks it's because everything else in our lives was so unstable after graduating from college - career, home, friends. We needed rules to understand our new place in the world, and since dating was top of mind at the time, that's where we focused. But another part of me thinks we were too bored and immature to think about anything else. When your job is to answer phones and transfer calls at an Internet company, you have *plenty* of time to write 500 words on how a man should approach a woman at a bar. After actual responsibilities enter your life, there's lifetime to deal with and worry about the bullshit of dating. You don't have time to dwell on it; you barely even have time to do it.

But when I re-read all those rules that I wrote almost six years ago, I see a person who was, above all, afraid, and fear breeds and need for order. The idea that there are no rules (a jerky pick-up line can be the start of a march toward marriage) or that you're better off trusting that you're the exception to the rule (he's just not that into you...right now) is often too much to bear at 22...or 27. It's not until you've experienced those rules working or not working or blowing up in your face that you realize the "rule" you should be trusting is your gut.

As it turns out, all those rules can get in the way of what's really right for you. It might not look "right" by the standards you set five years and 800 posts ago, but that's life. Messy, unpredictable, and totally unruly.

So I guess what I'm saying is that if you haven't read the 200 posts I wrote from 2007 through 2009, maybe don't. Then again there's some genius ideas about how to completely overhaul our entire dating system in there. They'd *never* work, but they're pretty clever if I might say so myself.

Ed Note: This entry technically is the reflection, so consider it one long "Ed Note." You're welcome.

Current Plans for my Future Rich Old Lady Self

from 6/17/13

I intend to be a rich old lady some day. This isn't a necessity - a, "life isn't worth living unless you're living large," thing, but I don't think it makes logical sense to aspire to be a poor, old lady, so I'm channeling my positive thinking toward a future filled with success.

So in an effort to "secret" my way into said success, I figure it also makes logical sense to have some plans for my future, rich old lady life. Here are those plans, to date. Suggestions are welcome from those of you who are or currently know a fabulous, rich old lady (ROL from here on out).

I'm going to get my hair done at least once a week.

I have really difficult hair, and I've never taken the time to learn to do it right. So when I'm a ROL I'm going to find a killer salon with super delicious smelling hair products and a fab gay man who will do my hair at least once a week. I'm not sure what kind of hair I'll have once I'm a ROL, but I'd like it to be like Jackie Kennedy's, so hopefully my future gay hairdresser will make it look like that.

I'm going to go to Europe at least once a year.

It seems like wealthy people spend a full season per year in Paris these days, so I'm going to join them for at least a small spell, annually. I think I'll change it up year after year so I can have really nice ROL scarves from all over Europe, but we'll see.

I'm going to have a small dog that I take everywhere

I feel like ROL's have small dogs that follow them everywhere so they always have someone/thing to talk at. Naturally R will be around to respond to my every magical old lady sentence, but when I go to places like the hair salon, I'll take my very small dog named something like Bernard or Angelo so I can continue to spew amazing lines about how to properly live life. That seems like the gist of what old people are saying most of the time.

I'm going to wear kaftans

Nan Kempner wore kaftans most days of her late life, and she looked fabulous, always. There's just something about a floor-length, Persian house dress that says both, "I have no where to go," and, "I've been everywhere." All of my kaftans will be bright, crazy colors and silk because I imagine silk is nice against wrinkly, old lady skin.

I am going to dine somewhere fancy on the same day at the same time every single week.

I briefly worked for the iconic movie producer David Brown, and he ate lunch at the 21 Club on Tuesday at 12:30pm (if I recall correctly?) every single week because, why not! I will do the same thing, but probably not at the 21 Club because it's a little stuffy there for me. If Momofuku is still in business when I'm a ROL (which, if I'm a really rich ROL, I'll make sure it is), then I think I'll dine there.

I am going to have an apartment in New York City

It doesn't matter where in the world I live permanently (if not, New York City), but I'm going to have an apartment in Manhattan once I'm rich and old. Of course, if I can only afford *either* yearly trips to Europe *or* this pied-à-terre, I don't know which I'll choose, but for now let's assume that I can have both. And if I can have both, let's assume that the apartment either overlooks Central Park or is near that perfect part of the West Village close to the Cherry Lane Theater.

I am going to have a room painted fuchsia

Diana Vreeland had a red room, so I'm going to have a fuchsia room. I think bright colors stimulate the mind, and you can't have a room that crazy until people don't care what you do anymore because they're just happy you're still alive.

I am going to only drink one kind of alcoholic drink, but I'm going to drink it at Happy Hour every day

By the time I'm an ROL I'll have someone else handling my driving, and hopefully everything else in my life, so I'll have plenty of time to enjoy an extra dirty martini, up, with Kettle One vodka every single evening. I might switch it up if my old lady palette prefers a Manhattan or maybe a very fancy French liquor, but for now let's say dirties and 5PM.

Ed Note: I find this list to be exceptionally complete, however I would like to add, "I am going to call everyone by ridiculous nick names because I won't be able to remember their real names." Ideas include: tootsie, pip, little lady, pumpkin/muffin/cupcake/strudel, lovely, lover, love, and bub.

The Final Word On: Hooking Up

from 7/11/13

I've decided to use up some of my remaining post space to soap box on the biggest issues facing 20-somethings today...*after* excessive college debt, rampant unemployment, and the astronomical cost of independent health insurance...

Hooking up - the catch-all term to signify intimacy of any kind, outside of a relationship.

You don't "hook up" once you're inside a relationship. I don't exactly know what you call the canoodling you do once you're in an actual relationship, other than *not* canoodling. I just know that it's called "hooking up" if you're doing it with someone that you absolutely do not call your boyfriend or girlfriend.

Here are my final, hopefully clear, mostly non-judgmental thoughts on the way the modern world has come to relate sexually.

- If you are hooking up because you want to hook-up, have at it. Your body is your temple. I hope that you are safe, respectful and mostly mature about it, but beyond that, go to town. I don't think there's anything wrong with expressing yourself sexually, experimenting with different approaches to your sexuality or engaging in sexual acts outside of a committed relationship. If it makes you happy, you are careful with your body *and* you are considerate of your partner, enjoy.

- If you are hooking up because you think you should hook up, take a pause. Peer pressure is a real bitch. We think we *should* lose our virginity by X age, try a threesome because that's being adventurous, or sleep around because we've earned the right. Sex is not a *should*. It's a *can*, if you'd like. If would *not* like for whatever reasons under the sun, don't. You're no less of a sexual being because you're not a "Samantha." Don't let any TV show or Cosmo article convince you otherwise. Do I recommend going through life afraid of sex? Absolutely not. It's a beautiful thing. But I'm afraid all the messaging around casual sex and hook-up culture is creating a generation of people who don't know that there's an option beyond following this trend. Just because casual sex (I'm including everything from a blow job to a threesome in "sex") is normalized doesn't mean it's normal. So if you don't feel like your normal self doing it, stop.

- This one is going to make you mad, but I don't care. I'm going to go out on a limb here and say that no man or woman was ever hoodwinked into a relationship via a hook up. In other words, if you are hooking up as a means to hook a man, you are wasting your time. Yes, you may end up in a relationship *after* having hooked up, but it won't be because of the hook up. So, if you're *only* hooking up with someone because you think it will convince them to date you, abort mission. I know. I've been there. "There" being a bar at 2AM talking to a drunk guy who is saying, "Just come home with me..." I'm saying, "How about I give you my number and we re-schedule?" (or something less cheesy, but, let's be honest, probably not). Then he's saying, "Why don't you want to? We've been hanging out all night." And so I go because I'm afraid that if I don't go, I'll never hear from this guy again. Guess what? I probably won't. Guess what else, that will be a blessing, and not even one of those tricky blessings in disguise. This is 2013. If he wants to find you again, he'll find you. You are not going to siren sex him into falling in love with you after one drunk lay.

- There is a fine line between hooking up with the same person for several weeks/months/years and being in a relationship with that person. That line is so fine, in fact, that some people can't see it. And unfortunately, the only way to make that line appear is to call it out directly. *Never* assume that just because you're exclusive, she's exclusive. And - though this is going to make me sound like a god-damned grandma - if you're too immature to ask the person you're sleeping with if they're also sleeping with other people, you're too immature to be having sex.

- And finally, intimacy may make you feel closer to a person, and in many ways you are, but hooking up creates a very specific intimacy. I won't call it false - that's not fair - but it can be incomplete if it isn't clear. Sex means different things to different people, but these days we often *have* sex in a manner that assumes it's all the same to everyone. Forgive that massive generalization (that makes me sound like a grandma, yet again) and just look out for yourself, no matter what you do.

That completes this afternoon special.

jessie rosen

The Final Word On: Dating

From 7/18/11

There was a time when this entire blog was centered on the topic of how to get dates, how to keep dating once you gotten a live one, and how to continue that dating pattern into a legitimate relationship. It wasn't until I actually completed that string of goals without following any of the advice I'd ever given anyone else that I decided to stop writing about dating quite so much. That said, I have some "bottom line" style opinions on the matter, and here they are.

- If you're not sure whether or not you're dating someone, ask them. If you're afraid that asking them will ruin your chance of actually dating them, you're right - it will.

- There will come a time when you have to decide whether it's better to be lonely *inside* a relationship or *outside* a relationship. In other words - would you rather have a bad boyfriend for the sake of having a boyfriend? I can't answer that question. I've lived it both ways through my 20s. But I will say this, there are boyfriends out there who are not "bad" at all. I know it's scary to hold out for those, but I also know it's impossible to get them if you're dating some other jerk.

- There is no definitive answer to the question of how long you should wait before you have sex. But from my dozens upon dozens of conversations on the topic I can tell you this, if the success of the relationship is relying on this issue, the relationship wasn't going to be successful.

- Be wary of people who say any of the following:
    - *I don't talk on the phone. I only text.*
    - *I can't sleep in anyone else's bed, so we have to stay at my place.*
    - *Nah. I haven't told any of my friends about us yet.*

- *I have this ex girlfriend/boyfriend who's completely obsessed with me.*
- *Sorry but I can't get off any other way, so...*

- I want to say something regarding on-and-off dating. I want to say that it's a bad sign about the stability of the future relationship or that it's indicative of issues or that it never turns out well, but I can point to too many stories that suggest otherwise. I will say this though: if you keep getting back together without figuring out what's going wrong every time you break up, you're going to keep breaking up.

- I support online dating. I've done online dating with some success, and I know people who've done online dating with ultimate success. But it is like anything else in the dating world - one way to meet people. Dating is a numbers game. Stack the odds in your favor.

- Meeting up with someone and their friends at a bar post 10PM is not a date. Call me old-fashioned. I take that as a compliment when it comes to dating.

And finally

- I don't believe that dating is dead, and I'm not sure it ever will be. But if I'm wrong and dating "like we used to" ceases to exist, it will be because we let it die. Every time we accept less out of our potential mates during that special time between meeting and making it official, less becomes accepted. It's nobody's fault, it's just human nature. We like to cut corners. I think it has something to do with the cave men. If you're fine with that, so be it. But if you want dating to be "more" than what you're experiencing, ask for it, require it, or wait for it to happen. I am not authorizing you to act like a princess (whether you're a guy or girl), and I'm not saying we need to turn back the clock on modern relations. I'm just saying that it's okay to want someone to pick you up and take you to dinner so you can have a nice, long conversation in private.

How To Survive Your 20's

from 7/10/13

After 826 posts (to date) and six years of writing on the topic of how to be a 20-something, I feel like I should end this epic (if I may say so myself) run by providing some form of getting-by guide. That's mostly because I can't get through a heart-felt "thank you and goodbye" post without sobbing, so a bullet point "how to" will have to do.

You should know that this started as a list of thirty five items, but the more I read them over the more I realized it takes very little to end up a happy, productive, debt-free 30-year-old, and that's coming from one who is sometimes unhappy, often procrastinating, and used to have a ton of credit card debt. What can I say? Do as I've learned, not as I've done? Nah. I had way too much fun to advise against making some mistakes. Instead I'll say, shoot for the following standards of living, and hope that fate, luck and a really good economy handles the rest.

Now, drum roll please…

- Spend less than or equal to the exact amount of money you deposit into your bank account every month. If you just read that and thought, "Yeah. Of course. How is that advice?" *Congrats!* You make enough money to live! If you just read that and burst into tears. *Don't panic!* Cut up all your credit cards, return and any all clothes recently purchased, and start over.

- Move out of your parents' house as soon as you possibly can, but not at the risk of blowing the above rule.

- Ladies, invest in one of those curling rod things. They really do wonders for the hair, and in no time flat! Gentlemen, please donate all of your giant, baggy cargo shorts to the Goodwill, or burn them.

- If you're still, "not sure what's going on between us," after three plus months, the answer is nothing.

- Call people - specifically your family members – as in, on the telephone, using your voice.

- If you don't know what the hell you want to do with your life, figure out some things you enjoy – hobbies not professions – and find time for those in your week. You'll probably stumble upon a career in six or so months. If you still don't know what you want to do with your life after six or so months, go to business school.

- Find a mentor, imaginary or otherwise. For example, mine is Nora Ephron. She was a very real person before she so sadly passed, but we never met and became best friends, as I intended. That has in no way stopped me from modeling my entire life against hers.

- Go on vacation with your best girl or guy friends as often as you can afford. Gchatting all day every day does not compare to spending quality time together reading *UsWeekly*'s out loud beside a pool in Puerto Rico.

- Never skimp on the following life products: things to make your skin look nice, one amazing set of lingerie, haircuts, bed sheets, dental care, high-speed Internet and birthday dinners.

- Learn to cook three dishes perfectly. This will fool any prospective partner for the time necessary to make them fall for you and will likely fool their parents for life.

- Remove any and all friends that you secretly hate spending time with from your life. I'm still not sure how to do this, but I think it involves not liking their Facebook updates or going to their birthday parties anymore?

- Invest. I'm not kidding. Put this book down right now and put whatever money you can spare into a 401K or Roth IRA or...those are the only two options I'm aware of at the moment.

- Develop an ear for your gut and listen to it at all times. Then develop an ear for when your gut is lying to you for "ulterior motivates" (wink) and listen to it *most* of those times.

- Watch all five seasons of *The Wire*. All of the most awesome people I know have watched all five seasons of *The Wire*, so I can only assume a direct correlation. I'm one down, so far.

- Think about if/when you might want to get married and/or have kids. You don't need to plot it on a graph, freak out about how far behind you are, then run out and freeze your eggs. Just don't forget to be aware of those ideas and goals.

- Print your photos. You'll thank me when the Internet dies.

- Take risks – lots of them – but don't make a fool out of yourself. If you're not sure whether or not you're about to make a fool out of yourself, ask a trusted friend or mentor. If they're not sure either, you are.

- Be the calmest person in the room - any room of any kind, all the time. People trust the calm person. People respect the calm person. People want to date the calm person. But most importantly, the calm person is calm, and that's really the only way to survive this mad world in one piece.

- Put your phone down and look around. This is not a metaphor.

- Stop drinking so much. I'm not going to put beverage units around that advice. You're an adult. Know when enough is enough.

- Just call him/her your girl/boyfriend already! What's the big deal? You're going to have to break up either way at this point, so just cut the crap.

- Know that most clichés are wrong, but these three are true: fake it 'til you make it, time heals all wounds, and, as a drunk gambler in Vegas once said to R, "after the fourth wife you've gotta' wonder if it isn't not so much them as it is you…"

- And finally, if you're hoping to transition from your 20's to your 30's with little drama, fanfare, or memory of everything you did wrong, don't start a blog like this one…

Ed Note: To those of you who have yet to enter your 20s, good luck, god speed, and I hate you. To those of you who are somewhere in the middle, I know, and I promise it's going to get better. And to those of you on the other side, is it me or is this a lot less miserable and a lot more exciting than I've been making it out to be for, oh, six years and 826 blog posts

ABOUT THE AUTHOR

Jessie Rosen is a writer.

She lives in Los Angeles. She's from New Jersey. She has an unhealthy obsession with avocados. She's working on some TV and film projects. She will soon marry the love of her life. She doesn't have a favorite color and never has. Her favorite movie is *Hook*, and she's not at all ashamed of that fact.

But for the purposes of ending this book with the point of the whole thing in the first place: Jessie Rosen is a writer.

Printed in Great Britain
by Amazon.co.uk, Ltd.,
Marston Gate.